MW01144695

Memoirs Of The Shkreli-Vata Family

Nush Mati Shkreli-Vata

Translated by the writer's daughter - Zina Prister

Edited and illustrated by the writer's great-grandson - Rob Emery

Memoirs Of The Shkreli-Vata Family

Written by Nush Mati Shkreli-Vata, in 1938-1942

Translated from Albanian in 1992-1994 by Zina Prister (born Shkreli-Vata)

Edited and illustrated in 2020-2021 by Rob Emery

Acknowledgements:

For word of mouth information, I am indebted to our mother, grandfather, uncles (Vuksan and Tomë) and Aunt Gjysto from our father's side of the family, and from our mother's side, to her uncles: Filip, Mikel, Lecë and Kin Çeka. I am also indebted to my sister, Ninja, who collected whatever she could of country songs, jokes, stories and customs of Malcija and of Geg (Northern parts of Albania).

Nush Shkreli-Vata
Shkodër, 1940.

Editing and illustrating this book was made possible using photos and information provided by my mother (Nina), her cousins, my grand-aunt (Zina), and various online sources, the most notable of which was the Marubi Museum [National Museum of Photography, formerly Marubi Photothèque]. I'd also like to thank my father (John), and grandmother (Ruth) who gave me a start in photography and art, which led to the skills needed to restore photos for this book. I used nine programs in my colourization process, the most helpful of which was developed by Jason Antic and Dana Kelley.

Rob Emery
Toronto, 2021.

Contents

Editor's Note & Photo Legend
By Rob Emery

The memoirs my great-grandfather (Nush) left us, that my grand-aunt (Zina) translated, provide a wealth of perspective on the origins of the Shkreli family and the life they led that I will always cherish. I had time during the COVID-19 pandemic to preserve them in digital format. I'd initially just planned to transcribe the text, but found it helpful to make edits along the way.

Nush and Zina often referred to the same person with different names: eg. nicknames and diminutives. For instance, Nine, Ninja, Nineta, Ninusha, Ninuška and Antonia were names used interchangeably with Nina. In Albanian writing, there are also different versions of each name when used with indefinite and definite articles, which themselves depend on the gender. To avoid confusion, as many people in the family also shared the same name, I settled on a unique name for people closest to Nush and left the alternates in square brackets, eg. Nina [Ninuška]. For Gasper, the name of Nush's father-in-law, brother, son, "cousin" and employee, there were no nicknames to differentiate them, so I used relation prefixes. For instance, "Baba" was used to denote a grandparent (though in Nush's case, it was his father-in-law, so he meant his children's grandparent). Nush sometimes wrote about relatives at a different level than actual: eg. his "Cousin Gasper" appears to be his cousin's son. I also updated the names of places. Nush, Zina and the maps often used place names from other languages and time periods, whereas I favored indefinite exonyms: eg. Belgrade [Beograd], Dubrovnik [Ragusa], Shkodër [Shkodra / Scodra], Vienna [Wien].

Some of the photographs in this book come from family albums. Others come from online sources and are only a best guess that they reflect the people referenced: they listed the same (or similar) name, and were taken in the same town as the people in the memoirs. The sources for the original photos are indicated with the caption marker, but I have since restored and colourized them. The colourizarion was done with an artistic, rather than historical, guess as to what colours things might have had. Places referenced in the memoirs have been highlighted in red on the maps.

[FA] - From the author's family's albums

[FAM] - From the author's family albums, photo by a Marubi [Marubbi] photographer.

[M1] - From the Marubi Museum, confirmed by family photos or other sources

[M2] - From the Marubi Museum, unconfirmed if it's the correct person

[PD] - From elsewhere in the public domain, confirmed by other sources

[S] - Stock photo, typically a modern photo

Introduction

By Zina Prister, with contributions from Nush Shkreli & Rob Emery

For future generations to better understand these memoirs, let's begin with the history of the region. Albanians [Arberians / Shquiptarja / Shqipëtart] are the descendants of the Illyrians and Celts, who may have established their rule in the Balkan Peninsula (southeastern Europe) even before the Greeks. The inhabitants of the Balkan Peninsula in this time were: Pelasgians, Thracians, Illyrians, Hellenes, Macedonians, Epirusians and Celts.

The Illyrians, and Celts, lived on the west bank of the Danube River [Donau], in Bavaria [Bayern], Upper and Lower Austria, West Hungary and the Alps [Alpen], up to the Adriatic Sea. On the Balkan Peninsula, they arrived around the 13th century B.C. and occupied the northern, western and southern regions. The east border may have been the Morava [Margus] or Drina [Drinus] Rivers, in Serbia. The Illyrian tribes that occupied the Balkan Peninsula were: Histri, Yasi, Yapodi, Liburni, Mezei, Dalmati, Breuci, Ardici, Autanati, Pirusti, Dardani, Taulanti and Peoni, etc. On the east coast in Italy, the Illyrian tribes were: Mesapes, Yapyges & Picenis.

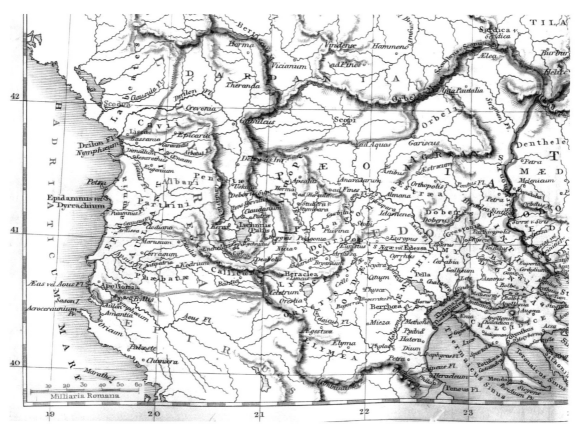

A Classical Atlas To Illustrate Ancient Geography, by Alexander G. Findlay, 1849.

Illyrians and Celts were Indo-Europeans and the documented ancestors of modern Albanians. After the defeat of the Illyrian King Gentius [Genthins / Genc], (168 B.C.), Rome annexed the southwest part of Illyria and made the rest part of their sphere of influence. However, the Roman conquest was not complete until the time of Augustus in 33 B.C., when Illyria became a Roman province.

The Illyrians played an important role in the Roman Empire. Many emperors were of Illyrian origins. The most prominent of them were: Claudius II, Gothicus, Decius, Aurelian, Dialetian, Diocletian (245-316 A.D.), Probus in the 3rd century A.D., Constantin The Great in the 4th century, and Justinian in the 6th century.

With the division of the Roman Empire in 395 A.D., Albanian ports became important trade centers. During this period, Durrachius and some other cities reached the height of their prosperity. As the power of the Empire declined in the 5th century, the Illyrian provinces were plagued by migrating and invading tribes: Vandals, Goths, and Huns in the 4th century, Bulgars in the 5th century, large numbers of Avars (who soon left to proceed towards Rome) and Slavs in the 6th and 7th century.

Slavs later began to penetrate Illyrian territories and the Byzantine Emperor Heraclius settled them in Illyria en masse. As a result, the whole region, except Albania [Arber / Albani], acquired the Slavic character it bears today. Faced with the danger of assimilation, the Albanians, who had by this time been converted to Christianity, moved southward. They concentrated mainly in the rugged mountain regions, where they remained under the rule of the East Roman or Byzantine Empire.

During the 11th and 12th centuries, Albania was overrun by the Normans and in 1190 A.D., during a period of Byzantine weakness, the Albanian Prince Progon established an independent state which lasted until the middle of the 15th century. In the 14th century, the Serbs conquered Albania. With the collapse of Stephan Dushan's Serbian Empire in 1355, Albania fell under the dominion of local feudal lords. The Topias and Dukagjinis ruled in the north and the Muzakas and Shpatas ruled in southern Albania.

The Ottoman Turks invaded Albania at the end of the 14th century. Under the resistance leadership of Gjergj [George] Kastrioti, the Albanians waged a struggle against the Turkish occupation from 1448 - 1466. Gjergj was born in Kruja, Albania in 1403, and was also known as Skanderbeg. When Pope Pius II launched the crusade to throw the Turks out of Europe in 1464, he arranged with the Alleats to crown this Albanian hero the King of Albania, because of his work in defending Christianity. With Gjergj's death in 1468 (with no descendants), the sun set on the Albanian nation and it became part of the Ottoman Empire.

Rembrandt sketch of Skanderbeg [PD]

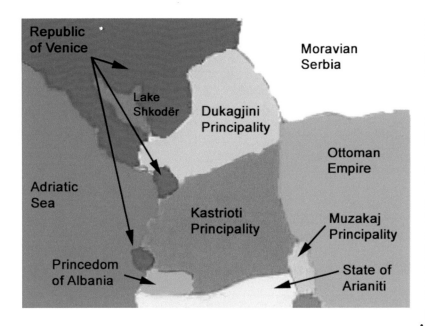

Map of Albanian Provinces in the 15th century, from Balkanian's Word [PD]

Many Albanians immigrated to Italy, Dalmatia (Croatia) and other parts of the world. Many who remained in the lowlands of Albania abandoned Christianity and converted to Islam. Muslim Albanians came to assume positions of importance throughout the Ottoman Empire. Although it was occupied by the Ottoman Empire, the Turks were never able to establish total control over Albania. Many Albanian leaders perished without leaving descendants except the family Dukagjini.

One of those descendants accepted the Islamic religion and went to Turkey, leaving no traces except for a well known poet named Mehmet Dukagjini. Another one, Kolë [Nicolaus], went to North Albania with his fighters and lived in the mountains. To deceive his enemies, he took the name "Kolë Pali" and his heirs took the name "Mark Kila" and "Gjon Mark", the name his family has kept to this day. These descendants of the princes of Dukagjinis passed on the law code of Lekë [Alexander] Dukagjini, that Lekë gave to the Albanians. After he left the province Dukagjini, Kolë Pali settled with his family and fighters in the province of Mirditë [Mirdita] and Pukë [Puka] in North Albania.

Lekë Dukagjini, from the General Directorate Of Archives [PD]

There was a large region in North Albania called Malcija [Malesia]. It included Major Malcija and Minor Malcija. The inhabitants of both were called Malcorë [and variants including: Malcors, Malissor, Malesor or Malisori in the international press]. After a couple of years of struggle with the Turks, the whole Malcija agreed to a compromise where the Malcorë acknowledged the sultan's sovereignty and the sultan acknowledged their autonomy. Through five centuries of Turkish sovereignty over Albania, the Malcijas maintained their independence, governed by semi-feudal native chieftains [bajraktars] and by the law code [Kanun] of Lekë Dukagjini.

Minor Malcija had six tribes: Kopliku, Grixha, Lohja, Rijolli, Reci and Suma.

Major Malcija had always played the more important role in Albanian history though. The five tribes from Major Malcija were: Hoti, Gruda, Kelmendi, Kastrati and Shkreli. Our family, Shkreli-Vata, are descendants of the chieftain of the Shkreli tribe. Feudal native chieftains ruled each tribe under their own banner and according to the highland law, the "Kanun" of Lekë Dukagjini, and a strong kinship organization.

In the 14th and 15th century, part of Albania was occupied by the Republic of Venice [Venetia]. Among other items, the archives of the Republic of Venice, "Acta Albaniae Venetae", contain a description of integral administration of Albania at that time: Volume No. VIII 1417 tax roll. These documents summarize the entire relationship of the family-tribe Shkreli [Skirelly, Skriely] with the administration of the Republic of Venice.

During the latter part of the 18th century, several native princes rose to prominence. From 1775-1796, the Bushats ruled the Shkroder Duchy, extending their authority over North and Central Albania. From 1790-1822, Ali Pasha (1741-1822) ruled the Duchy of Janina, which extended from Vlorë and Berat to Çamëria [Chameria] and Thessaly.

Painting of Ali Pasha Of Janina by Seymour Stokes Kirkup [PD]

The Albanians have little recorded history over these long centuries of Roman, Byzantine, Slavic, Venetian and Turkish domination, as the Ottoman domination over Albania was more stern than in other parts of their influence in Eastern Europe. They destroyed as many of the records of Albanian history, and forbade teaching the Albanian language and history in schools. The Albanians emerged from relative obscurity only in the 19th century. The rise of modern nationalism was delayed longer than elsewhere in the Balkans. At the end of the 19th century, nationalistic sentiment awakened.

When Austria occupied Bosnia and Hercegovina (1878), Albanians had hoped Austria would occupy Albania too, and so free it from the Ottoman Empire. At that time, there was no discussion of Albanian independence. The League For The Defense Of The Rights Of The Albanian Nation [The League Of Prizren] was formed in Prizren [Prisrend, Perzrend, Prizreni] in Kosovo to defend the Albanian territories which were under the occupation of the Ottoman Empire. Accordingly, the League sent a note of protest to the European powers at the Congress of Berlin to protect it from land grabs from its neighbouring nations: Montenegro, Serbia, and Greece, but it did not initially ask for the freedom of Albania or even more autonomy. The League's goals evolved, and it waged a heroic struggle for autonomy from Turkey.

Members of The League Of Prizren: Ali Pasha Shabanagaj (sitting front left), Haxhi Zeka (front middle) & Bajraktar Kadri Bajri (sitting front right). [PD]

Meanwhile, at the beginning of 1894, there was a local conflict brewing between the Catholics and Muslims in the Malcija mountain region of Rrjoll [Rrjolli / Rijolli, near Maranai]. One morning, they found all the crosses on the graves broken in the church's cemetery. The cross is a symbol of Christianity, and was a deeply respected sign among the Malcijas. If you curse or swear the cross to a Malcorë, they would shoot you (it was often the cause of blood feuds in those days). The Malcorë of Rrjoll, and other Malcorë joining in, revolted against this barbaric act, maintaining that this insult could only be washed away with blood.

They came down to Shkodër [Shkodra / Scodra / Skadar / Scutari] and assembled a commission in Gibal to discuss the problem, including Muslims and Catholics of Rrjoll. The Muslims denied the charges, declaring that this must have been done by their enemies to instigate a quarrel. This was a complicated situation, and to make it worse, important. While they were trying to solve this situation, another came up. In the mosque in Rus (a large area in Shkodër as you enter from the Malcijas, just south of Dobraç), the hodgia [Muslim priest] entered in the morning to find the mosque stained with blood and intestines of a pig, with the head and legs of the pig at the place from which the hodgia speaks. He sounded the alarm, and Muslims hurried to see what had happended. When they reached the mosque, they stood petrified seeing the mosque so desecrated.

They revolted, and shouted that the mosque had been stained with blood and so it must be washed off with blood, and so they set off to massacre the Catholics. The Catholics got scared, and shut themselves in their houses. The more reasonable Muslims halted their people, telling them it was their enemies that did this, to put more discord among them. They ordered schools immediately closed, and sent the children home. The priests gathered in the Roman Catholic Archbishopry for consultation. Both Catholic and Muslim districts individually gathered to discuss the matter. They were all armed.

The Muslim party in Shkodër, which was more liberal and reasonable, started to calm down the masses, telling them that they should wait and see what the Vali-Pasha of Shkodër would say [Pasha is a Turkish honorary title appended to the names of military leaders and governors of provinces and Vali-Pasha or Valia is the pasha of a town]. Meanwhile, the order was given to close shops and the bazaar [pazar / bazar], and stop all contact between Muslims and Catholics. This order surprised those in the bazaar, as they didn't know what had happened yet. Shkodër became a dead town with nobody in the streets.

A large number of Muslim families took to defend Catholic families, who were their friends, or were in danger, so that no Muslim dared to attack those families or else unleash a vendetta with the Muslim family that had given their word, their "besa", to protect them. The common people went to take refuge in the houses of important and powerfubl Catholics, as their houses were larger and better protected by high walls. Word of this event spread rapidly through the villages and Malcijas.

Hearing about it, armed Malcorë headed to Shkodër to defend their brothers, and the diplomatic corps sent urgent telegrams about these events to their respective countries. The Ottoman authorities in Albania took security measures. The army was readied and reinforced their positions. The cathedrals and Roman Catholic churches hoisted flags of his Holiness the Pope and that of Austria (during the Ottoman occupation, the church in Albania was under Austrian protection). The diplomatic corps told the Vali-Pasha he would be held accountable if anything happened, so he gathered the members of the country council to discuss the situation.

"Tak-tak" - gunfire was heard.

The armed Malcorë were already near Shkodër when the Archbishop Monsignor Pasquale [Pascal] Guerini, sent his secretary and some priests to intercept them. They were ordered not to enter Shkodër until they heard again from the archbishop.

The Malcorë were led by their priests and among them was Don Lazer Mjeda [Don / Dom are an honorific title given to clergymen], who later became archbishop. Don Lazer [Lazër / Lazaro / Lazarus] Mjeda [Miedia], after he spoke with the archbishop's secretary, addressed his men, saying that in the name of Jesus Christ, they should stand down to not make matters worse.

Don Lazer Mjeda [M2]

The Vali-Pasha of Shkodër asked the Muslim and Catholic eminences, presidents of districts and municipalities, and the bajraktars and dukes of both Malcijas to come to him. It was a huge meeting. After consulting about all the details of recent events, they came to a decision to satisfy both sides: the crosses on the graves in the churchyard of Rrjoll would be replaced by new ones by the Ottoman authorities, some of the Catholics and Muslims from Rrjoll would be put in jail, the mosque would be repainted, and a couple of lambs would be sacrificed at the reopening of the mosque. At that ceremony, the army, the authorities and other Catholics would join the Muslims, along with music.

For a time, the army kept order in Shkodër, and more bloodshed was avoided. The poor people suffered the most, many losing their jobs. Because of this, well-to-do Catholic families organized the distribution of provisions to all those in need. As the Ottoman Empire grew weaker by the day, the Balkan occupied nations tried to free themselves from the Turks completely. The Great Powers of Europe infiltrated the region with their propagators and agents. Each of these wanted a larger sphere of influence in the region. Each of the small Balkan nations also wanted to expand.

After France's influence in Albania diminished in 1870, Austria took its place. Austria was the protector of the Roman Catholic Church in Albania, and sustained all the clergy. Italy wanted to spread their influence in Albania too and that annoyed Austria. Although Italy wasn't as big a state as it is now, it succeeded to get an agreement called the "Golukovski - Venosta Contract" signed with Austria. According to this contract, nothing could be done in Albania without mutual consent between Italy and Austria. However, many times, Austrian officers in disguise would visit the mountains of Shkodër to learn strategic positions and meet with the Malcorë, their bajraktars, and the clergy of those areas to organize an uprising against the Ottoman Empire, and then get Albania to ask Austria for help. Many Catholics from Shkodër participated in this conspiracy.

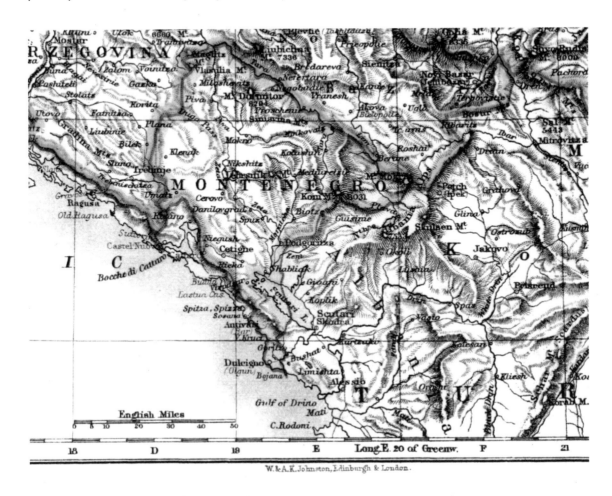

Map Of Bosnia, Serbia & Montenegro, Adams Antiques 1897.

In those days, especially in the Malcija regions of Kastrat [Kastrati], Hot [Hoti], Gruda, Kelmend [Klementi] and Dukagjin [Dukadzin], the parsons were Franciscans, mostly from Venice. Although they were subsidized by Austria, they were Italian and secretly informed the Italian consulate in Shkodër, who informed their government in Rome about these activities. Roman officials asked the Austrian government in Vienna [Wien, Austria] for an immediate explanation: "What do they mean by a revolution in Albania". In Vienna, they were surprised that their secret activities had been discovered, and answered to Rome that they hadn't the slightest idea what this was all about. At the same time, the Government in Vienna got very angry with the members of the Albanian mission who were organizing this scheme, for their indiscretion.

At the time, Austria had good relations with the Ottoman Empire. To protect those relations, Austria ordered their ambassador in Istanbul to inform the Ottoman Government that the Malcorë of North Albania were preparing an uprising against the Ottoman Authorities. They were advised to take steps in advance before the revolt breaks out, as Austria didn't want unrest there as they were the protector of the Roman Catholic Church in Shkodër. It was a diabolical move.

The authorities in Istanbul immediately sent orders to the Vali-Pasha of Shkodër to find out what was happening in the Malcijas, and to take adequate security measures. The Vali-Pasha summoned the Muslim and Catholic eminences from Shkodër for consultation. The Malcorë, according to the agreement they had with Austria, waited for the promised supply of arms and ammunition. Meanwhile, the Ottoman authorities started rounding up some eminent people from the Malcijas, and interning them, and so the uprising failed.

The Malcorë, angry that the Austrians had betrayed them, composed a mocking poem about their deceitfulness. The poem's first verse goes:

"Oh Austria, oh you who... what did you do
with the twenty companies...
Kola was forwarding warning letters,
but he did not know that the Franciscan priests
in the Malcijas did not know how to read them..."

The reference here was to Kol [Kola] Serreqi (grandfather of Nush's wife Nine) as the Serreqi [Sereggi] family was in the Austrian clergy. Austria was not idle. It's policy was to prevent any union between Catholics and Muslims in the region, by any steps, however wicked. Besides Austria, there were Balkan nations that did not want this union either, as it would make Albania stronger. Austria's aim was to gain ifluence, and organize things in Albania, in such a way as to conquer it for itself. To achieve this, they first needed revolts and unrest in the area, so more shootings, and casualties, occured between Muslims and Catholics.

Sultan Abdul Hamid II [PD]

Istanbul, under the reign of Sultan Abdul Hamid II, wanted to give a concession for

13

the trans-balkan railway to be built along the river Drini, in North Albania, to Shkodër. Austria wanted to keep Albania underdeveloped and in obscurity so that they could easily occopy it, like they did Bosnia and Herzegovina [Hercegovina], and then build the railway themselves. Twice the sultan made the proposition for it to build it through Shkodër, and both times with the help of Austria's collaborators in the clergy, it was rejected. No need to write about the prosperity and progress it could have brought to Shkodër, and Albania.

At that time in Tiranë, there were steps being taken toward the liberation of Albania from the Turkish occupation. These were arranged by the Albanian family of Toptani. Gani Bey Toptani ruled in Tiranë, Shijak, Javaj and Durrës. He had supreme power over those provinces and was greatly feared by those who respected the Ottoman Authorities as he hindered their activities. The Turkish family Yellej opposed Gani Bey Toptani, but he succeeded in forcibly sending them away (some to Greece, and others to Istanbul). The sultan in Istanbul gave the order to transfer Gani Bey from Tiranë to Istanbul. It was not easy to accomplish, as in Tiranë, Gani Bey had the support of most of the population, and it was a relatively independent state within a state.

Gani Bey Toptani [M1]

The Pasha of Shkodër invited Gani Bey to pay him a visit in Shkodër, telling him he could bring as many escorts as he wanted. So Gani Bey arrived in Shkodër with his heavily armed escorts and was free to move about. From that time, a friendship formed between his family and ours. One day the pasha invited him to a banquet at his house with other guests, like he had many times before. Gani Bey's armed escorts were being entertained in another part of the house. Later, it was clear that all that happended had been meticulously planned in advance.

A couple of military units were ready in their garrison, for any eventuality if there was any resistance. Gani Bey's escorts were disarmed. Some of the young strong soldiers were in readiness to quickly disarm and capture Gani Bey. After the guests had finished their meals and were drinking coffee, the soldiers swiftly stormed in, disarmed and captured Gani Bey. He tried to resist, and called his escorts, but it was in vain as they were already captured too. Seeing his resistance was futile, he said to the pasha, "This is the besa of the Anadols?" (The pasha was a Turk from Anandolia). It was an evil thing to betray someone, especially a friend, while they are a guest in your home.

Gani Bey was well guarded until the arrival of the steamship from Istanbul two days later. A well armed company escorted him to the ship. Soldiers from Tiranë, who happened to be in the army in Shkodër at the time, wanted to try to liberate him, but he had sent word not to risk their lives over it. He had many friends in Istanbul and hoped that the matter would be resolved when he arrived there.

When he arrived, he was summoned to an audience with the sultan, and after he gave his besa that he would not leave Istanbul, he was set free. One day in a Constantinople club, he got in a conflict with the son of the sadrazam [Sadrijazem / the Grand Vizier], where he slapped the son because of an insult. The police wanted to arrest Gani Bey, but he had a gun in hand and did not let them approach him. The entourage of the son of the sadrazam was enraged, and plotted Gani Bey's murder, which they carried out a few days later.

The Albanian residents in Istanbul revolted and wanted to avenge his death, but Gani Bey's widow and his brother Essad Pasha took that upon themselves. Gani Bey's soldiers and escorts in Tiranë all wanted to go to Istanbul and sacrifice their lives to avenge their Bey [leader]. As only one could go, they drew his name blindfolded. It was Xhise Faje, who was the uncle of Mustafa Krues.

Essad Pasha Toptani [M1]

Xhise Faje armed himself with two guns and waited for a suitable moment to kill the sadrazam or his son. On the 7th of October 1899, when the son was driving through Galata Bridge (in Istanbul), Xhija stopped their carriage, and mortally shot the son and his friend. Xhija was immediately captured, and the sadrazam asked for the death sentence. Since Turkey had abolished death sentences, he could only be sentenced to life imprisonment (or 101 years, as it was called in Turkey). His luck was that in 1908, thanks to the new constitution, he was set free with the other prisoners. The Turks got more apprehensive and since then started to be more agreeable and willing to satisfy the Albanians.

There was a folk song composed about this event while he was imprisoned:

"Sadrijazem akulltarë Ç to desht pushka me Shqyptar Mos u tut Sadrijazem Mora gjakun e zotnis t'em.	Sadrijazem, you intelligent man... Why did you need a shootout with the Albanians? Do not get scared, Oh Sadrijazem. I only took vengeance for my lord.
Mos me kjaj e shkreta nanë Se jam ritë neper Toptanë Mos me kjani grue e fëmi Se jam rrit me bukë te ti."	Don't mourn my poor mother, As I grew up among the Toptans. Don't mourn my wife and children, As I grew up on his bread.

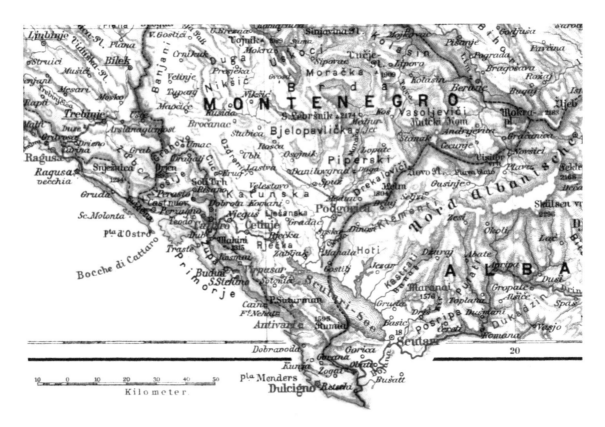

Montenegro (& Albania) Map from Meyers Konveraltions - Lexikon, 1906.

In 1909, the Congress of Dibra was formed, a meeting organized by the Young Turks party with the hidden intent of persuading Albanians to abandon their nationalist movement and the recently approved Latin-character-based alphabet. Instead, strong opposition was voiced at the meeting and it was established that the Albanian language could be taught freely with any alphabet. Other concessions included tax reforms, and the right to keep bearing arms.

The Albanian Revolt Of 1910
From La Trinuna Illustratata [PD]

On November 28th, 1912, in Durrës [Durcë /
Durrësi / Durazzo], after a series of revolts against
Turkey, Albanian patriots led by Ismail Qemal,
Luigj Gurakuqi (our father's first cousin), Hasan
Prishtina, Isa Boletini and Don Nikoll Kaqorri,
proclaimed the country's independence. The
former Ottoman province of Albania became an
independent country. At the London conference of
December 1912, the Great Powers recognized
Albania's independence.

However, the 1915 demarcation by a special
commission appointed by the Great Powers excluded a large part of its territory from
Albania, including Kosovo and Çamëria. More than a third of the Albanian people
ended up outside its borders. During World War I (1914-1918), Albania became a
battlefield occupied at different times by various belligerent powers. The Paris Peace
Conference in August 1920 finally recognized Albanian independence. At last an
Albanian government was established with Tiranë [Tirana] as the capital in 1920.

Yugoslavia &
Albania from Cram's
Unrivalled Atlas of
The World, 1920

Chapter 1: The Early Days

Albania was divided in two parts: North Albania, where the Gegs [Ghegs] lived, and South Albania, where the Tosks lived. Major Malcija, in North Albania, had five tribes: Hoti, Gruda, Kelmendi, Kastrati and Shkreli, each led by their chieftains, called bajraktars, with their own flag [and military unit, called bajraks]. The chieftains were recognized by the authorities in Shkodër, on whom they depended. They had special privileges, and governed by the law code Kanun [Kanuni] of the Prince Lekë Dukagjini. This legal code was applied by the verdict of the elders of the clan [selected individuals sworn into the position] in parts of the country where there was a lack of schools, communication, military, courts of justice or civic administration.

The people of both Major and Minor Malcija were known as Malcorë (mountaineers). They were famous for their heroism and benevolence. Each tribe covered several provinces, and their leaders were often succeeded, son after son, starting with the oldest. If there were no sons left, successorship went to the oldest cousin. The provinces had leaders called dukes, who were subordinate to the bajraktars. The dukes were also succeeded by their sons. The provinces also had elders [counsellors]. The dukes and bajraktars relied on these elders to confer and make decisions on matters of justice, punishment and settling disputes, as well as answering to the central authorities in Shkodër. The bajraktars and the dukes led their fighters in defence of the country, or on occasion to represent them in Shkodër.

The Shkreli tribe covered four provinces [village & surrounding areas]: Vrith, Dedaj, Bzhetë [Bzheta] and Zagorë [Zagora]. The territory of the tribe extended from Veleçikut Mountain (east of Hoti), along Prroni i Thatë [Pronit Thatë] Valley to Shkodër Lake [Scutari-See], and at one time encompassed about 30,000 people. The tribe was initially Catholic except for several Muslim families. Most of the Shkreli people were tall, like all highlanders, and proud of their Malcorë origin, their splendid national clothes, silver and gold chains, watches, other jewelry, amber pipes set in silver filigree (an ornamental handwork of fine silver and gold wires, that looks like lace), as well as of guns and rifles (decorated with silver, mother of pearl and ivory), and their thoroughbred horses. In short, they had beautiful attire and often caught one's eye.

Prroni i Thatë River Valley [S]

18

In 1830, when the Ottoman authorities in Shkodër became more liberal and asked for a representative of the chieftain of the tribe Shkreli in Shkodër, the Bajraktar, Marash Vat Dashi Shkreli, sent his youngest son, whom he considered the most capable of handling this task. He was our grandfather, Vat Kol Vata Shkreli [Vata / Vatë]. His wife was Mrika Matush Tome, daughter of the Duke of (the province of) Dedaj.

As the Duke of Vrith [Vrithi, Vrithë] had no son nor successor, the Bajraktar of Shkreli had appointed his third son as Duke of Vrith. Vata, the youngest son of the bajraktar, often had to go to Vrith (northeast of Koplik) or Shkodër as his father's representative. Because of this, Marash decided Vata should take up residence in Shkodër. So the bajraktar bought and provided his son with: a house and property in Shkodër in the street of Gjuha Dolë, near Shkodër Lake, complete with meadows for the livestock he had also provided. He also had built vineyards, and houses for shepherds, servants and horses, in the regions of Ana e Malit [south of Shkodër] and Bardhanjort [Bardangolt] fields (east of Shkodër).

1839 Tribes of Albania Map from Bulletin De La Société De Géographie, 1841.

Our grandfather moved to Shkodër with his family consisting of: his second wife Mrika [Maria], three sons, Vuskan (age 15), Mati [Mathew / Matija, age 5], and Tomë [Tom / Toma, age 3], a daughter Nusha (age 6), and his grandson Ndocë [Ndoc / Anthony, age 18]. Ndocë, was the son of Vata's son Kol [Kolë / Nicola], and Drande [Rosa], both now deceased. Drande was the daughter of Lulash Prekë, who was the son of Duke Matush Leka. Grandfather's house was the headquarter for meetings of the tribe Shkreli, so rarely was there a day without guests. Besides looking after the interests of the Bajraktar of Shkreli, grandfather also took care of his own property and interests.

Until his children came of age, grandfather kept them all close. When he moved to Shkodër, he sent them all to schools. There were no public schools, only private ones. He was lucky, as at that time, Don Peppino and some others got permission from the Turkish authorities to open a school in Shkodër, teaching in Italian, as well as Albanian. They enlarged it every year, especially when the Jesuits took the directorship of the school. Our father and our uncles all attended this school.

Besides the four grades of elementary education, there were 8 grades of gymnasium with classical courses, or 4 grades of special courses for elementary school teachers, and 4 grades of special courses of a commercial nature. The the children of the upper class of Shkodër went to this school, and it produced the intellectuals of Shkodër. The teaching was meant to be in Albanian, but most classes were in Italian, as the Jesuit teachers were Italian. Learning the Italian language was very useful at that time, as Shkodër was closely associated with Venice.

The clothing for the upper class men at that time was: brandavek-sharvadha (a kind of wide trouser of red cloth with gold and black cords), a silken sash (with a leather holster for a gun or two), a fez (red felt cap with a silken blue tassel), enteri (a waistcoat with sleeves) and xhamadan (a sleeveless wool waistcoat / over-shirt). The latter two were embroidered with golden threads and cords.

Although part of the Ottoman Empire since 1497, the Malcijas were never under Ottoman administration. Major Malcija and Minor Malcija had their own code of law. Each bajraktar ruled their own tribe. They didn't have a right to their own army, but neither did they have to supply the Ottoman army with their boys. Although the Malcijas had these priviledges, they still depended on Shkodër with regard to trade and food going in and out of Albania, as well as for international relations. Both Malcijas had an agreement with the Ottoman authorities: leave me in peace if you want to be left in peace. Despite this, during the 500 years of Ottoman rule, the Malcijas revolted many times.

There was much unrest in Shkodër. Because of gross injustices, the common people rose in arms against the Turkish authorities and the vizier's ruling party. The viziers [vezirs / vizirs / wazirs, high ranking political advisors] had great priviledges and made the people pay high taxes. Hamza Bey Kazazi [Hamz Agë Kazazi], from a respected and well known family in Shkodër, appointed himself as the leader of the people's revolt. The Malcorë also took part in this revolt. Our grandfather, with agreement of the Bajraktar and the Dukes of Shkreli, gave Hamza all the support he needed.

The revolt against the Turks in Shkodër started in late spring, a time when the sheep were sheared. The custom on that day was that the owner of the herd had to entertain not just the whole family, but also many friends. They had all ridden from Shkodër to the part of the mountain where the sheep were kept. The servants, with necessary items and food, had gone there earlier so they could prepare a banquet and reception with the help of the shepherd's wives. Roasted lambs on a spit were traditionally required.

Sheep farming in northern Albania [S]

On the first day of shearing, the master cut a handful of wool from the sheep, as a sign for the shearing to start. After this ceremony, the shearers would work on the sheep for several days, keeping many shearers busy. Next, the master of the house, our grandfather Vata, took his friends and family to where the banquet was prepared. When the feasting was over, an older relative named Lulash Prenka, who was an expert in looking at and interpreting the bones of the lamb's shoulder, took the shoulder bone, put some salt on it, made the sign of the cross, and started to examine it. After a while, he turned to Vata, as the sheep's bones could only foretell of its owner, and told him about family things, good and bad, health, destiny, property, and finally about the current situation.

"The situation is very serious and it won't be long in Shkodër (before the fighting will start)". Everyone looked at grandfather, who remarked that it could not be, as when they had left Shkodër that day, all was calm. The older man persisted. After that, grandfather left the dining room with his guests and after washing their hands (a whole required ceremony of its own), went out to where coffee was served. They hadn't even finished their coffee when a rider arrived, informing them that Hamza Bey Kazazi had started the fighting against the Turks.

As grandfather had given his "besa" (word of honor), he said to those men present: "Let us go and help them. Today is our day to win or perish!". All the men took arms, sent word to their tribes, and mounted their horses to ride to Shkodër. These men included our grandfather (Vata), grandmother's cousin (Marash Gjoka) and even our father (Mati), who was still very young but rode after them. The other riders, absorbed in their thoughts of the fight, did not see him until it was too late to turn him back. They stopped at Kazazi's residence to meet up with Hamza and the other Malcorë that had gathered. They left Mati there with the Kazazi family, who did not let him go until Vata came to fetch him. Since then, the grandsons of Vata have always been close friends of the Kazazi family. Due to the revolt, the common people of Shkodër gained the rights they demanded from the vizier.

As the years passed Vata's wealth increased. He invested in livestock, wool, olive groves, walnut tree groves, chestnut groves, leather and, to a lesser extent, in cereals and vineyards. At that time, the commercial connections were only with Venice. His export products were: wool, leather, walnuts, chestnuts, timber, and wood. As long as grandfather was alive, the exports of the whole family Shkreli-Vata were sold under his name. At first, he and his sons only imported needed items, and exported Albanian products, but later as more roads were built, they also exported imported products. In the beçistan [bedesten, a covered market building in the commercial district], they had large warehouses with: wool, leather and articles imported from Venice. Vata still had his property in Malcija, as well as the property of his wife in Vrith. He always spent summers with his family in the mountains of Vrith.

According to the customs of the time, our grandfather Vata first married off his daughter Nusha [the diminutive of Prendusha]. Nusha, being the only daughter, was supplied with a rich dowry and jewelry. She married Tonin [Anthony], son of Marc Lufi. (Sr.), from a well known and ancient family in Shkodër. Per the code of law of the Malcijas, as long as the father was alive, the sons owned nothing. After his death, they divide the property. The girls did not inherit anything. It depended on the brothers if they wanted to give them something. If there were no sons, only daughters, the property would go to the nearest male cousins. Because of this, the parents always tried to marry off their daughters before the father's death so they could give them a dowry. Brothers, except for some characterless ones, never married off a sister without giving her a proper dowry. The family honor was at stake, and the brother that did not give a dowry for his sister was despised by the rest of the family. This code of law was abolished around 1935 during the reign of King Zog I of Albania. With the new law, daughters gained the same rights as sons in the division of property, as well as the right to vote in elections.

Nusha had three children: Çile [Çilja / Cecile], Leze [Lezina / Zina / Therese] and Mark [Marc Lufi, jr.]. Çile married Çin [Augustin] Bushati, and had two daughters. One married Ndocë [Anthony] Lexhen, who graduated from Vienna University (Austria), and the second married Mark Çurçia. Leze became a home nun (home nuns are special nuns, never marrying but having special rights in the house and society, conceded only to wealthy Albanian girls). Marc never married. He fell in love with his cousin's wife, but could not marry her so didn't marry at all. Neither did he work, as he inherited his father's estate.

King Zog I of Albania, 1939. [PD]

Mark Lufi, jr. [M2]

Vata's eldest son, Vuksan, married Zef Lufi's sister, Lena [Helena]. They had two sons and a daughter: Cin [Augustin], Gjush [George] and Kusha. Kusha married Kolë Zojzi and had two sons: Ndreka [Andrew] and Cin. Ndreka married the daughter of Filip Kroqi. Cin, the older son of Vuksan, married an Italian from Udine (Italy), named Corina. His parents were against the marriage but our father Mati, and Filip Paruca persuaded Vuksan and his wife to approve the marriage. Mati and Filip had often visited with Corina's family, and later became Cin's best men. Cin was a very clever man, and a great mathematician. Cin and Corina had two sons: Cirio and Sokrat. Cirio died very young, but Sokrat is still alive, and in Shkodër.

Vata's grandson Ndocë [Ndoc / Anthony] was first married to Drande [Rosa, Dan], the sister of Zef [Joseph] Kraja and the aunt of my wife Nine. He had a son with her, named Kolë. Kolë left Shkodër after his father's death, and went to live in Ismir (Turkey), where he married a Greco-French girl. My brother Kel and I went to see him in Ismir in 1902, as Gasper (our brother) had done earlier. Ndocë remarried after his wife's death, to a woman named Cina, the daughter of Kolë Berdica. His brothers were against the marriage as they considered the Berdica family unsuitable. Ndocë and Cina had a daughter named Angje [Angela, but they called her Ganxhe], and two sons: Zef and Gasper. Zef became a well known priest [Don Zef].

Sokrat Shkreli [FAM]

Their Gasper married Kusha, the niece of Pjeter Çoba. Gasper's family were against this marriage and because of that, he moved with his wife from Shkodër to Cetinje (Montenegro). My brother (Kel) and I met him there when we participated in the wedding of Prince Danilo of Montenegro [Danilo Aleksandar Petrović-Njegoš], as guest of King Nikola I of Montenegro. Later on, their Gasper and Kusha moved to Trieste (Italy). I met up again with Gasper, in Trieste, in 1911, and Kel met him again in 1912. They died without any children.

Ganxhe married very young and soon after, her husband died. According to our customs, because she was childless, she had to return to her parents. The second time, she married Shan [Marc], son of Gjon Markshteja. They had two sons and a daughter Rosa. Rosa married Gjon, the son of Hil [Michael] Gega. The sons did not marry.

Uncle Tomë, the quietest of Vata's sons, married the daughter of Kolë Hallaba, Çile [Cecile]. She was quiet too. They had a son, Kola [Kolë], who being an only child, was spoiled, and had no interest in his father's business. He often travelled, and went to Ulcinj [Ulqin / Dulcigno, near the mouth of the Buna river]. There he met Tina, the sister of Franco Pici. Although his parents were against this marriage, Kola married

Tina. At first the family was angry, but later they reconciled. Kola and Tina had a daughter Çile, and a son Tom. Çile married Pjeter Kodeli in Durrës (Albania) and Tom married the daughter of Gjon Shestani from Shirokë (near Shkodër) who was also the niece of Kolë Vasa.

Gasper Shkreli [M2]

Kusha Shkreli [M2]

Shkodër was the centre of commerce, not only for North Albania, but also for Prizren, Gjakova [Gjakovic], Pej, and Kosovo, Macedonia, and Rumelia. Shoker, being near the Adriatic Sea, along with Tivar [Antivari] and Ulcinj, were the link between east and west. The port of Shëngjin [Shnjin / San Giovani di Medua] was built later. Shkodër was the center of trade from the west all the way to Adrianopol [Edirne, Turkey] and Filipopel [Philippopolis / Plovdiv, Bulgaria] in the east. This lasted until the Skopje-Saloniki railway line was constructed, which made Saloniki (Greece) an important port for trade. Until then, a caravan of 200-500 horses used to arrive in Shkodër every day from far away tribes, loaded with: wool, leather, carpets, ropes, silk, timber, game, cheese, walnuts, hazelnuts, plums, prunes, apples, pears, etc.

Those looking at Shkodër today wouldn't believe the great role it once played in trade and transit. Although it had no industry, Shkodër was well known for its trade. Grandfather's sons, as well as those of Uncle Vuksan, already grown by now, enlarged the business with Venice, Kosovo, Macedonia and Istanbul. Shkodër had a great reputation, not only for the quality of goods, but also for their clean and honest trade. At one time, trade and commerce were only allowed to be carried on by wealthy people. When the railway line to Istanbul openned to traffic, through Hungary, Serbia and Bulgaria, and the second line openned, going through Skopje [Shkup] to Saloniki, that took away all the importance from Shkodër, and reduced the once great city to near the poverty line.

Shkodër cathedral construction, 1858-1867 [PD]

Chapter 2: Death In The Family

Grandfather Vata had a very important political and social position, not only, because of his wealth and as the representative of the tribe Shkreli in Shkodër, but also because of his sons and grandsons. They were all grown up, industrious, without vices, and of good character. He felt very strong, powerful and content. The whole family was in a good position. Alas, as the years passed and old age crept in, he had to discuss who would succeed him. Which of his children was decided by the members of the elder council. The position was always given to the most capable son, and this decision had to be obeyed according to the code of law of Lekë Dukagjini. Because of that law, Vata confered with his brothers, the Bajraktar of Shkreli and the elder council. Our father Mati, though he was second oldest, was the most capable of the brothers, so the council decided he should take Vata's place in directing the family after his death. His brothers did not oppose this.

After his death, Vata left his sons not only his wealth, but a powerful position and influence in political and social circles. Our father Mati frequented the Jesuit college in Shkodër, and his father sent him to Venice for further studies. The management of the family's immovable property was given to our Uncle Vuksan. The management of the family's trade was give to Uncle Tomë. The representation of the interests of the Shkreli tribe, as well as travel that was needed outside of Albania, to Italy, or to Istanbul, remained Mati's duties.

Our grandmother, Mrika, was a very clever, reasonable and energetic woman. She supported, guided and helped her sons a lot. Maybe you, young children, while reading this will wonder that a woman at that time would have had such importance since in those times, they were seldom asked their opinion. Well, this was not the case of women from Malcija, as they always stood side by side with their husbands and sons.

Mati proved that he was the right choice with regard to his responsibilities. He had to travel a lot, on business as well as for pleasure. Both his brothers and a nephew were already married, but not Mati. Many matchmakers sought to change that, but without success. Finally, in 1857, when he became 30 years old, he married Leze [Lezina / Zina / Theresa], the daughter of Frano Gurakuqi. Her mother Tone [Antonieta] was the daughter of Pjeter Çeka. Leze was 18 years old then and not only from a known family, but also beautiful, clever and energetic. His brothers and our grandmother, Mrika, were happy that he was at last married and had made a good choice.

Our family Shkreli-Vata in Shkodër was not only powerful by itself, but even more so being from the family of the Bajraktar of Shkreli. There was a saying, "The brother of seven hundred brothers". The families Çeka and Gurakuqi were powerful too by themselves. As the saying goes, "A good lad with many friends": the families bound by marriage with other powerful families increased their prestige and became stronger. Mostly, this was the purpose of these families marrying each other.

When our father Mati got married, there was a big wedding. The whole family was invited, as well as friends in Shkodër, and other tribes in Malcija. Our father was already friends with Leze's cousins, of the Çeka and Vasa families, and this friendship grew stronger. The marriage of our parents was a happy one, with harmony and reciprocal understanding. After his early death of a heart attack, which was a very painful loss, a great sorrow fell over our family. Mother often used to speak the best about him, and we loved her very much for this.

The families Gurakuqi (with a house on Parucë street in Shkodër) and Çeka (in Perash, the Catholic side of Shkodër) had their origin from Mirditë in North Albania and were Malcorë. Frano and Tone Gurakuqi had three children: Ganxhe, Leze and Gjon. Ganxhe married Shan [Mark] Vasa. They had two sons, and two daughters: Ndocë, Cin, Gjyste [Josephina], and Shota [Elizabeth]. Ndocë, after he graduated from the college of Jesuits in Shkodër, was taken by his Uncle Pashko Vasa [Vaso Pasha / Wassa Pasha] to Beirut (Lebanon), where Pashko became the Governer, under the reign of the Ottoman Empire and Sultan Abdul Hamid II. Shan and Pashko were the cousins of our mother, and so we also called them uncles. In Beirut, Ndocë went to college again. Later, his uncle sent him to Istanbul to the sultan school for diplomacy. Had Ndocë not died so young, for sure he would have succeeded his uncle, who went on to become a famous politician and writer.

Pashko Vasa [Vaso Pasha], 1878 [PD]

Pashko Vasa's first wife, Nine, was from Shkodër. Together, they had a daughter who married an Armenian Catholic lawyer, named Kupeljan. He was from Beirut, and they later moved to Istanbul, where they had two daughters: Rosa and Sylvia. Their mother died when they were children. Because of his daughters, Kuplejan never married again. Pashko Vasa lost his first wife as well, and remained on good terms with his son-in-law. The second time, Pashko married a French lady, named Madame Berta, against the wishes of his family. We, being the family on his mother's side, didn't visit him anymore.

They had two sons, Kel and Shan, who became good, honourable men. Although Madame Berta never visited Shkodër, offended by her husband's family's opposition to their marriage, her sons did several times. They always stayed with us and we befriended them as cousins. Their Kel died young, just before the beginning of WWI, in Rome from a heart attack. We lost touch with Shan after WWI, and last we heard we was in Istanbul.

Gjyste Vasa married a French engineer named Shneider, and had a daughter named Sabina. Shota died in Bruse (Turkey), unmarried. Cin died in Shkodër, unmarried. So, the whole family of Aunt Ganxhe and Uncle Shan Vasa ended without offspring. Uncle Gjon, after he finished his studies in Shkodër, was sent by his father to Venice to complete his studies. A couple of years later, as he was preparing to return home to Shkodër, he died of a heart attack. This was a very painful loss for the whole family. His sisters were very fond of him. Our mother, could not bear to hear the mention of his name after his death, nor did she go to any parties if it was the feast of Saint Gjon. With his death, the masculine line of the family of Frano Gurakuqi was extinguished.

The Çeka [Çeka-Summa] family had powerful influence in the political and social scene. Their family was a go-between in matters of protection of the inhabitants of Shkodër, and civilian and military administration of internal affairs in peacetime, and international affairs in times of war. I was well informed about the occurences in the house of Çeka as our mother's grandfather and her uncles were close friends with our father Mati, even before he married their grandaughter. Their house was always open, as they entertained a great deal of family members, Malcorë, friends, representatives of civilian and military authority, and church dignitaries. They had a chapel in their house for ecclesiasticals to serve a mass for the occupants.

Pjeter Çeka senior had three sons and a daugher: Ndocë, Filip [Philip], Mikel and Tone. Ndocë married Drande [Rosa], the sister of Teresa Stefes Bianki and they had two sons and a daughter: Pjeter, Lecë [Nicola] and Mrika [Maria]. Pjeter marrier Leze, daughter of Loro Radovani, sister of Gjergj Radovani, all part of an ancient Catholic family in Shkodër. Uncle Pjeter had no children. Uncle Lecë married Çile, daughter of Pashko [Pascuale] Çoba and sister of Pjeter and Zef Çoba. They had two daughters, Rosanna (who married Pashko Kakarriqi), and Nine (who married Simo Shuli), and a son Tony (who married the daughter of Kolë Lufi). Mrika was an only daughter, very beautiful, clever and kind. She married our mother's cousin Kin Gurakuqi. Tone married Frano Gurakuqi.

Our mother's uncle, Filip, the second son of Pjeter Çeka senior, was mostly engaged in mediations and interventions. Accompanied by influential Muslims, he represented the Catholics of Shkodër in meetings with the Ottoman authorities in Shkodër. Filip was often a member of the council of municipality. He married Teresa, daughter of Gjerg Gurakuqi, sister of Peter Gurakuqi, and aunt of the cabinet minister Luigj Gurakuqi (1879-1925). Luigj, along with Ismail Qemali [Ismail Kemal / Ismail Qemal Bey Vlora], on the 28th of November in 1912, proclaimed the independence of Albania and hoisted the Albanian flag in Vlorë [Vlora]. Luigj was assassinated in Bari (Italy) in 1925. It was rumoured to be by the Tiranë government and others, because of his political convictions and activities.

Rosanna & Pashko
Kakarriqi [M2]

Our mother's uncle, Mikel
Çeka, had a powerful
political influence in
Shkodër and Mirditë. His
first wife was Çile,
daughter of Filip Kraja.
They had a daughter, Dan
[Drandofile / Rosa], who
married Loro Lufi. His
second wife was Tina,
daughter of Palok Shiroka.
They had two sons and a
daughter.

Meanwhile, back on our
father's side of the family,
things were going well until
the revolutions started to
interfere with my father's
duties, and prevented him
from travelling to perform
his obligations. The roads
at those times were not
safe, and all goods, people and property were transported by caravans for protection.
Each of our father's brothers already had their own children, and gradually,
misunderstandings, mistrust and rivalries started to build between then. Because of
that, the brothers decided to separate and divide their wealth and businesses.
According to the customs of the day, brothers lived in separate buildings, but
together in one complex. Our father Mati was upset by this decision, as dividing them
would diminish their power and influence. But, his brothers insisted, so they
summoned the family council, and the wealth was divided and everyone went their
own way.

For our father, it was easier now, as he only had to take care of his immediate family,
as well as the interests of the Shkreli tribe in Malcija. Mati was an energetic and
religious member of the church councils, and supported them generously with
donations. He had a strong desire to see Shkodër connected by railway, as he knew
that would bring prosperity, but the proposal was rejected by the majority in Shkodër.
He could never understand why the others didn't see the profit Shkodër would gain
from the railway.

After he separated from his brothers, and could make his own decisions, Mati
decided to establish a silk factory in Milan (Italy) with Pjeter Gurakuqi. They bought

30

the silk cocoons in Albania. At those times, Albania had a rich silk trade and exported a great deal of cocoons. Father used to spend a lot of time in Milan, not only for business, but he and Pjeter had a good time there too. During the winter theatre season, he had a regular box in the theatre, La Scala [Teatro alla Scala], as he was very fond of classical music. He was interested in arts and paintings too. Our house in Shkodër became full of Italian furniture, china, ceramics, paintings and many other fine art objects. But to our regret, all this got lost, as well as the house, during the bombings of Shkodër in the Balkanik Wars, in occupations and in fires. Often, when I think of how our house was once full of beautiful and valuable things, remembering those times breaks my heart. They would have been great souvenirs for our children, and helped them understand their grandfather Mati's way of life.

La Scala Theater [S]

Shkodër was full of antiques which we did not appreciate, probably not realizing their value. Foreigners, on the other hand, made good use of this ignorance and took advantage of buying these for next to nothing, or receiving them as gifts, or requisitioning them during the occupations of Albania. When Albania achieved independence in 1912, museums opened up in Shkodër, but to our regret, many of these antiques had already been lost.

Our father was very interested in books. It seems he had been a liberal (a rarity in those times) and had brought back from Italy many valuable books by free-thinking philosophers. After his death, our mother's confessor, under false pretenses, visiter her and asked to see the books in the pretence of checking if any of them were on

31

"The Index" (a list of books banned by the Roman Catholic Church). After seeing them, and feigning that most were on the Index, he took the books with him to his monastery, making believe that he was going to burn them. When I grew up and took an interest in Albanian history and language, I realised how valuable the books were, that we'd lost in a foolish way. Among these books was the book of the Roman Catholic Archbishop of Skoplje, written in Latin and Albanian [Shqyp]. He wrote about the religion and the people from the area. People who write dictionaries in Albanian, often take this book as the basis for Albanian words which are no longer in use.

When father Mati went to open up a silk factory in Milan, he had a trusted employee take care of the business in Shkodër. Meanwhile, our mother took care of the estate, arable lands, vineyards, orchards, olive groves, walnut groves, and livestock. The personnel, field labour, farmhands, and other staff turner to her for any problems that arose, and informed her of their achievements. This was good experience for our mother, as she was well trained in administering to the estate when our father died, and she had to take on everything, as the childred were too young and still at school.

When our father was alive, none of his employees dared to cheat or deceive in their management duties, but after his death, there were many occurrences. Father was looking forward to the day when we three sons would become his right hands, and help in managing the estate, trade and factories, etc. as it was far too much for him alone. Often he had to leave the managing to strangers, which frequently led to large losses. All these losses did not upset him, as he considered himself very lucky to have three sons, and a daughter. He used to say to our mother, "Three sons and the hope to get a good son-in-law, my dear Leze, our hearts are full".

Mati was a very kind and loving father. Whenever a son was born, as per the customs of the day, the men in the family fired guns in the garden or from the windows. They fired guns, rifles, and even muskets as a sign of celebration. After the initial surprise from the noise, friends and relatives hurried to our house from the pazar (a street market held regularly, an outdoor bazaar] to congratulate and drink a cup of coffee (a sign of good luck in those days).

Our parents had children before us, but they died in infancy. Of the surviving children, the eldest was Ninja [Nine / Antonia]. At those times girls were not as welcome as boys, but father loved Ninja just as much. He celebrated her name day every year as solemnly as he did for the boys. She was named after our grandmother, from mother's side, as the name of our grandmother from father's side had already been given to Uncle Vuksan's daughter. Ninja obtained an education, even though girls at that time were not allowed to go to school. Teachers (Tina Nikës, Kush Micia and Tereze Berdica, and later some Jesuit professor) came to our house to teach her, and our parents gave her all the opportunities. Four years after Ninja, Kel [Mikel / Michael] was born, a healthy handsome boy. Four years after that, Gasper was born. After him came a girl, but she died in infancy. I, Nush [Francis / Frances], was born in 1880.

When father was alive, we were a happy family and never imagined we could lose each other, least of all that we'd soon lose our father. Father was very diligent, but he also liked to enjoy life, and led an interesting one. He had travelled a lot to Western

Europe, as well as to the east: Istanbul, Aridanopel, Filipopel (Turkey), Beirut (then Turkey, now Lebanon).

We used to go as children to the mountains of Vrith in the summers, as Vata had done. The mountains of Shkreli [in the Shkrel municipality of Shkodër county] were known for years for its good air. To go to Malcija, you had to go on horseback as the paths were too narrow for carriages. When we visited Major Malcija, and I went to stay in the residence of the Shkrelis, we drove in our carriages until the bank of the river Buna [Bojana], then we (men, women and older children) had to mount horses. The little children were put in baskets made for this purpose. The baskets were put on a horse, one on each side of the horse. Then other horses were loaded with necessities and gifts. Servants guided the horses with children, things and women afraid of riding. This is how the caravans were formed. In front of the caravan rode two servants, then followed the men, women, children, pack horses, and servants.

The national costumes were so beautiful that the caravan following the serpentine track in the mountains was a wonderful sight. To reach the residence of the Shkreli's, it took us 4-5 days. Of course, these trips were always planned and prepared in advance. Two of our bodyguards (boys), went in advance to the place where we would stop for lunch, and to the next place where we would spend the night. Until the end of World War I, it was customary for men of importance to have several young men from their tribe accompany them as bodyguards wherever they went.

In every village, the ruling leaders of the village always had guest rooms to receive friends and special visitors, because at the time, there were no hotels, except "hans", where people of no importance would stay. The youth, of the house we would stay at, would ride towards us to meet us and pay homage. They similarly saw us off on our departure, following until the end of the property, where the youth from the next house we'd stay at were waiting to meet us. And so this would continue, until we reached our tribe. These homages would be made to every caravan that belonged to the house of the bajraktar or dukes of the tribe (it would have been a great offence to not do so). Of course, wherever we stopped, worthy gifts were given to show the respect we had for the house. The tribes, or provinces, which the Bajraktar of Shkreli was not on good terms with, we avoided.

We got the greatest welcome when we arrived at the border of the Shkreli tribe. There, two or three people from each province and the youth of the bajraktar's house were waiting to meet us. They accompanied us to the house of the bajraktar, while shooting in the air, as a celebration to welcome their cousins. We went very often when we were children and early adults, but seldom after marriage. Then the Balkan Wars started, and then World War I, and these customs began to disappear.

All our servants were from the villages of the provinces of Shkreli. When they got married, either they stayed with us or returned to the village and others came in their place. The boys, who were our bodyguards and took care of our father and uncles, and later, us brothers (Kel, Gasper and Nush), were from the best families of Shkreli villages as it was a priviledge to take care of the cousins of the bajraktar. Although they were not paid (as they were considered members of the family), when they left, they got gifts which were more valuable than if they had been paid. When the lords were preceded by two bodyguards, enemies would not dare attack them, as they would have entered into a vendetta with the boys families, because of the offence caused to their lords, which was their responsibility. These vendettas, involving the male members of the family, were practiced in many countries in Europe.

In Shkodër, father had a dominant position as an executive of the Malcija for the clan Shkreli, and attended many meetings, including representing the people's committee before the Ottoman authorities in Shkodër. He often opposed the orders of the Ottoman authorities, when he thought that they were a heavy burden on the people, and that was the main reason people appointed him. He had great influence among both Muslims and Catholics in Shkodër. Of course, all these positions and duties were without pay (until World War I, after which it was required). They were considered an honour (only the wealthy and powerful could afford to be appointed to these unpaid positions).

Mother used to tell us how father believed in people's honesty. Whenever anyone came to him in distress, he would lend this person the needed money without a written receipt. Just a shake of hands would do (in those days, this was pledging your word). There were those that never returned the debt, especially after Father's death. The gallantry of those times was different. Loans were given in secret, so as not to embarrass the borrower.

Father became unexpectedly ill, with heart problems. The doctors found that it was angina pectoris. Although he immediately stopped performing his regular duties, his heartbeat was already weak. It didn't last long, as on the 17th of November in 1886, he died, and was buried a few days later. Before he died, he said his goodbyes to his relatives, then to his wife, and then to us, the children. It was a very emotional and sad moment. He praised our mother and recommended we always follow the path of honesty and truthfulness. Even so many decades since then, as I write these words, I hear the voice of dear father and feel his hand on my head.

Chapter 3: Life Goes On

Father's death was a very painful and unexpected event. It was the first time we'd faced the realities of life and death. His burial was a grand one. Besides the family, friends and clergy, there were also authorities of state and other important representatives of the Malcijas in attendance. Father's history ends here, may he rest in peace. Then, a life without our much needed shepherd started. Mother, energetic and clever as she was, knew that she had to get accustomed to living her life without father's guidance. After the first few days of pain and grief, she took the lead in the management of our house and estate. We children were all still in school and too young to help.

First, she liquidated the silk factory in Milan, because she assumed that leaving it in the hands of strangers so far away would have been a bad idea. Then, in Shkodër, she liquidated the merchandise that was in our import-export warehouses, with the intention that they would be reopened when her sons finished their studies and could run the business. She left only the warehouses in which the goods were from our estate, for export to Venice. These included: wool, leather, nuts, wood, swine bristles (used in making brushes), and other things of less importance.

Kel was the oldest of the sons. When father died, he had already graduated from the economic branch of the Jesuit college in Shkodër. This school was for upper class citizens; sons from the lower class went to the Franciscan school. After Kel's graduation, mother sent him to Italy to improve his Italian language skills (though nearly all the subjectes were in Italian at the Jesuit School too). After Italy, she sent him to Istanbul for a year to improve his Turkish language skills (though this language was taught in Shkodër too). When Kel completed all his studies, the elders of the clan Shkreli appointed him to succeed his father as the representative of the Malcija Shkreli before the Ottoman authorities in Shkodër.

Kel, though a little nervous, took father's place in all social and political activities. He was young, full of energy and enthusiasm, good-hearted and diligent. He soon distinguished himself, not only in speaking, but also in writing the Turkish language. During the Ottoman Empire, a person who spoke and wrote the Turkish language had "Effendi" appended to their name, so Kel was "Mikel Effendi".

At that time, the governor of Shkodër was Mustafa Sim Pasha [Pasha is a title of military leaders and governors of provinces], who held the rank of marshal [myshyr]. Beside the Muslim members, Filip Çeka, our mother's uncle, was a council member of the Municipality of Shkodër, from the Catholic side. The Ottoman Empire often took sons of distinguished Muslim families in Shkodër and sent them to school in Istanbul to prepare them for important positions afterward as pashas or viziers. Sometimes they took a capable and intelligent Catholic from a distinguished family too. Uncle Pashko Vasa was one such person.

The governor, knowing that Filip was our mother's uncle, had called him to speak to our mother and persuade her to let Kel go to an Istanbul school, the Mekteb-i Sultani (a famous school). All men of importance and in diplomacy came from this school (including Uncle Pashko Vasa). It was a great honor for the family for their son to be asked, but mother could not let him go. Her view was that if he left, it may have been permanent (as it was with Pashko) and she could not bear him being so far (at those times, with travelling done in caravans and stagecoaches, distances seemed even greater). They tried to persuade her of the benefit to her son, but it was in vain. She thanked Mustafa Sim Pasha for this honour, justifying herself that she had recently lost her husband and didn't have the heart to let go of her eldest son. Mustafa Sim Pasha was a good man, a real gentleman. Powerful as he was, he could have ruined our family for this decision of hers, and the affront. But Mustafa, on the contrary, understood and admired our mother, and supported Kel on all occasions.

Kel Shkreli [M1]

Mekteb-i Sultani [PD, Source: Abdullah brothers]

Gasper, our brother, completed his commercial studies at the Jesuit College in Shkodër. At first, he didn't want to continue his studies, he preferred to reopen our father's import-export business. Because of that, our mother sent him to practice some of this trade with merchants in Shkodër (our cousins) and in Venice (former friends of our father) before she let him start his own business in Shkodër. On the 5th of May of 1894, the big warehouses of the Shkrelis, that had been closed after father's death, were reopened.

The post service of the Ottoman Empire performed its duties only inside the Empire. The official commercial and personal mail going out of the Empire was undertaken by the Consulates of Austria (+Hungary) and Italy on established days. The mail inside the Empire was transported by caravans of horses, the leader of which was called "Tatari". We had large warehouses for storage of goods when they arrived until they were needed by the merchants in Shkodër, as well as in Kosovo and Macedonia. Besides the warehouses, we had shops, and a factory for cigarette paper. I nearly forgot to write the title of our commerce business. It was "Gasper e Fratelli Shkreli" (Gasper & Brothers Shkreli).

Gasper showed great ability in managing the family's commerce. Introducing himself to the owners of big commercial firms in the east as well as in Western Europe as a son of Mati Shkreli-Vata, he was accepted by all of them with confidence, which is very important in commerce. The business bloomed. Like father, Gasper had to travel a lot to Venice, Trieste, Istanbul and later Vienna. It gave mother great satifaction seeing him follow the political and social path of his father, and succeed in business.

No need for me to write, as my children when reading these pages will have already found out, the world is not as one would wish it to be. Seeing that the sons of Mati, although young, were matching their father's success led to much envy, jealousy and plotting. Many times we were distressed and had to innocently bear the consequences of these injustices. It would not have surprised us if these had come solely from our enemies, but sadly, they also came from relatives and former friends. My dear children, I am not going to write about these events and name names. Unpleasant and sad things are better forgotten.

Our sister, Ninja, was the only daughter and was loved by the family. She was tall, like most Malcorë women, timid, good-natured, sensitive, and soft-spoken. For us, she was a beautiful flower. In addition to her education (which was unusual for girls), she also became skilled in embroidery, drawing and painting. Many of the patterns she needed for her embroidery, she drew herself, and chose the colours. At those times, girls and women used to embroider and do needlwork for recreation if they were from wealthy families, or for a living if they were poor.

When father died, Ninja was ready for marriage and had many suitors. Father hadn't wanted to marry her off young, so she could be with the family for longer. After mourning father's death, mother and Kel, as the oldest son, started to choose which of the suitors would be best for Ninja. Ninja declared that their choosing was in vain, as she had decided to become a house nun. Mother and Kel tried to dissuade her, but Ninja theatened to go to a convent if they persisted.

House nuns retained the right to inherit property from their parents, as well as take part in management of their affairs after their passing. They no longer had to cover their faces with a veil, as other women did in Albanian towns (whether Catholic or Muslim), excluding the Malcijas and smaller villages (where the women didn't). This veil custom started in the 16th century and lasted until 1912). In 1930 King Zog I of Albania forbade Albanian women from going out veiled.

As much as we were sorry we did not gain a brother-in-law, we were happy to have Ninja with us. She was a great help in the house and in the garden, as she was fond of flowers. After mourning our father, our house was openned up again to continue our hospitality and entertain guests as it used to be when our father was alive. Although mother did not feel like doing it, heartbroken as she was, she did because of the political and social position our family had.

Ninja became like a brother and accompanied us to all the meetings and festivals in the Macijas, of our and other tribes. She travelled with me to Venice and Istanbul where we had close relatives. For many years, she collected folk songs, and ballads of Malcijas that were sung at weddings, engagements, name days, and handed down from generation to generation by word of mouth. They were stories, tales, poems, proverbs, usually anonymous and often had many versions.

I, Nush, was the youngest child (born the 6th of May 1880). When father died, I was 6 years old. I missed father more than my brothers did. There was a big difference growing up without his guidance at my age compared to my brothers who were 11 and 13. Maybe as the youngest, I was more attached. I still remember that his passing away led to deep sorrow.

At school, I was good and completed all my studies. Like Kel, I did commercial studies at the Jesuit college, in Italian and French. After that, I was sent to Italy to perfect my knowledge of both languages. When Gasper reopened the warehouses, I was 14 years old. Although I was still young, Gasper and Kel made me their partner.

Nush Shkreli-Vata [M1]

Kel was engaged with the Ottoman Authorities, and was an orator. I, on the other hand, was a writer, and performed nearly all of Kel's correspondence with the Ottoman authorities. Later on, I accompanied him to the official and social meetings. Although I was still at school, Gasper also gradually left me to tend to his bookkeeping and correspondence. Often Ninja helped me as she was sorry seeing that I had no time for relaxation and entertainment.

Mother, sister and we three brothers were very close, bound by a rare understanding. Mother, a widow with four children, seized the management of the house with all her energy, and authority. Her comments and discipline ensured we never dared do anything without her approval. She wanted to put us on the right path for our future. She also took part in the selection of our friends. We did not only love our mother but we also feared and respected her. Not only while she was alive, but even after she left us, we followed her advice and example.

Besides our duties, we had fun too. Rarely was there a night without guests. We celebrated name days with banquets and music, with a group of 6-10 musicians with violins, sazes and flutes (it was common for people of importance to have that while entertaining). Besides name days, there were festivities for the New Year and Carnival. Celebrations were often held when important people visited Shkodër, like relatives of the Macija that stayed with us for a while. We also attended the festivities given by other families.

Once a year during the summer, we visited our tribe Shkreli in Malcija. In spring, there were festivities about shearing sheep. At the end of summer, there were festivities at the time of gathering of grapes, and other festivities which required the presence of landlords. As you see, although there were no cinemas or other kinds of modern amusements, we had plenty of entertainment. We were all very social, had no financial problems, were healthy and young and we thought that our style of life would last forever.

Our families had good relations with the Archbishop Monsignor Pasquale Guerini and the clerical party, and often entertained them as courtesy required. At that time, Kel and I were the only eminent people in Shkodër that spoke and wrote the Turkish language, which is why we had more connections and friendly relations with the Ottoman Authorities. The clergy both from Shkodër and the surrounding areas asked for interventions from Kel in whatever dealings they had with the Ottoman Authorities.

The population of Pukë [Puka] was a mix of Catholics and Muslims. One day, there was a conflict between them in connection with the church. Pukë was in the durisdiction of the Bishop of Zadrimë [Zadrima]. The priest of the Pukë's parochy came to Kel with their problem, and brought documents that showed the church was in the right. In Shkodër's court, Kel convinced the judges that there was injustice done towards the Parochy of Pukë, and the case was ruled in their favor.

The Muslims did not like that Kel defended the Catholics, even though we only intervened when we knew that we were on the side of justice. They suspected that the case was only ruled in the church's favor because of the friendship they had with

39

Kel and our family. They wanted to stop his further interventions, so they submitted a strongly worded accusation to the Pasha of Shkodër against Kel.

Because of this accusation, the pasha assembled all the members of the provincial council. Pjeter Çoba was a member of the council at that time. He was a relative of ours, as his sister married Lec Çeka, our mother's cousin. After the council meeting, Pjeter Çoba came right away to our house to inform us of the accusation. Pjeter said he's stood up at the meeting and declared that the accusation was false, and submitted the documents that the original ruling was correct. The pasha realized that there were no irregularities, and in private advised Pjeter to not expose himself so openly.

Ali Bey Qyrti was from Kurdistan [Bey / Bej / Beyg / Beg / Begum and assorted alternatives are a title meaning chieftain of a region]. He was the son of Bedrim Pasha, the chief of the Kurd clan, and had 72 brothers and sisters. Bedrim rebelled against the the sultan, was defeated, and was caught by the Turkish army. As punishment, his family was scattered to different places in Turkey. Ali Bey Qyrti was interned in Shkodër with his family. When he arrived in Shkodër, he came to pay us a visit. After that, our families became good friends.

He had two wives (allowed by the Muslim religion), the second of which was a very good friend to our sister (Ninja). Although he was confined to Shkodër, he had his own escort, and his word had unlimited power. Maybe it is more accurate to say that he was distanced from Istanbul. He didn't get along with the Muslims in Shkodër, as they were loyal to the sultan, and it seemed Ali Bey Qyrti had a grudge against the Turks and Istanbul, because the sultan had dispersed and destroyed his clan.

At that time, the general commander of the gendarmerie (a military force with law enforcement duties) was Mehmet Pasha Terhalla. He had come to Shkodër from Tetovo (Macedonia). He was an Albanian from a well known bey's family in Kosovo. The major of the gendarmerie was Ilmi Bey, from Shamit in Damascus (Syria). Together with Ali Bey Qyrti, they formed a triumvirate, always together. Ali Bey was interested in justice and whenever he saw injustice, especially against the Christians, he interevened with such vigor that nobody dared to oppose him. As our families were good friends, many people came to us to implore us to have Ali Bey intervene on their behalf.

Ali Bey Qyrti [Ali Shami Pasha] [M2]

40

But, as we succeeded to do good for one side, we also made enemies on the other. Many times we got passionately involved in things that were not our business, to help those in need. In those times in Albania, it was the custom for families of influence and power to help the common people. It was considered the honour of the house, as Malcorë inherited that responsibility for others, and we were known for this. As the saying goes, "a happy man can get anything done".

Something unusual happened in the Malcija region of Kastrat. Some Muslim families in Shkodër were granted a concession from the sultan: as a reward for certain services, they could tax the Malcorë of Kastrat on goods brought to Shkodër for trade. The parson of the Parochia of Kastrat was Father Luigi. Because of this situation, he came to Shkodër and asked Kel to meet him in the convent of the Franciscans in Gëjuhadol (part of Shkodër). He begged Kel to get Ali Bey Qyrti to intervene. They went to Ali Bey's home, who told them to return in three days with the bajraktar, the elders of the clan and some important people of Kastrat. Meanwhile, Ali Bey went to the Valia [what they called the governor of a town], to inform him that Ali had asked tne leaders of Kastrat to come and that the Valia should order the gendarmerie not to obstruct their entrance to Shkodër.

The Valia was greatly surprised, as the concession was from the sultan so he could not change it. Ali Bey tried but failed to convince the Valia to send a telegram to Istanbul, so they could cancel this concession, as it would cause more headaches for the Ottoman Empire. Kel was in a dilemma about what to do as it was bad to go against the sultan's wishes, but it could also be bad if the Malcorë whom he had encouraged started a conflict. He decided to send the telegram himself.

Two days later, the Kastrats arrived, led by Father Luigi. Father Luigi, the bajraktar, and the elders of Kastrat entered Ali Bey's house. The others waited outside. The people of Shkodër were surprised to see the Kastrats enter Shkodër freely, knowing about the sultan's order. Ali Bey and the Kastrats went to the Valia, who received them with honours, thanking Ali Bey for his efforts to correct this injustice as a good patriot. From that day, the taxation concession was rescinded as a good will gesture from Istanbul.

The Muslims of Shkodër did not like this. They were accustomed to having things done their way, and constantly complained about Ali Bey to Istanbul, saying he constantly interferes in civilian matters and should be transferred out. They petitioned to Tahir Pasha and Halil Bey (sultan's guard), who convinced the sultan to transfer Ali Bey to Bitola [Bitolj, Macedonia], and after that, to Janina (Greece). He wasn't there long either, as he got into conflict with the Pasha of Janina, and was returned to Shkodër.

We were very glad for him to be back. He had two sons, Saledin Bey and Kadri Bey. They returned to Shkodër just in time for the celebration of "Madonna of Shkodër" (the Virgin Mary Our Lady, patron saint of Shkodër). This feast is celebrated with religious ceremonies, festivities, fireworks, and banquets in every house, according to their means. Guests come from all parts of Albania. On the eve, and the next day (always the third Sunday in October), Ali Bey, his family, and Hamdi Bey joined the other guests, as they had never seen this festivity being celebrated in a Catholic house. We had many guests from both Malcijas, and among them were Muslims too.

According to the customs of Shkodër, whoever knocked at the gate of the house and said that they had come to Shkodër to celebrate the Feast of Madonna was let in. Those guests were accommodated according to their ranks. On the eve of the celebration, the feast was greatly enriched by folksongs, and dances. In the evening, Kel and I (as Gasper stayed with the guests) went to pay a visit to the Catholic Archbishop of Shkodër as the courtesy was required. He invited us and our important guests to come the next day and watch the religious procession from his balcony.

Ali Bey continued to interfere when he saw injustices, including one time when he took the army's side and caused the transfer out of the Valia (Pasha of Shkodër). Eventually, Ali Bey got promoted to brigadier general and was transfered to Istanbul. The new Valia was a civilian named Rashad Pasha, and had an Armenian civilian aid, named Agap Bey. Agap Bey was a Christian. Every Sunday, he came to church and took part in the festivities and services. He and his family became friends with ours. It came easily for us, as we three brothers spoke and wrote Turkish well, which was rare among the Christians of Shkodër.

Nush Shkreli (left) [M1]

In 1901, when in Istanbul, Kel and Gasper were guests of Ali Shami Pasha [formerly called Ali Bey Qyrti]. Kel and I also visited and were his guests in 1902. It was the first time I went with Kel on a longer trip towards the east. We went from Shëngjin (the port for Shkodër at the time) by steamship via Corfu [Qerfoz], Piraeus [Pireas] and Athens to Istanbul and Ismir. We stayed a month in Istanbul. It was a pleasant surprise for me, seeing so many interesting places and things. We had a good time visiting the families of Aunt

Ganxhe and Uncle Pashko Vasa. We were invited and visited with Tahir Pasha, and Hamid Bey of Kraja. He and his men kept guard of the sultan's palace [Saraj] and of the Sultan Abdul Hamid II.

We stayed with Ali Pasha for 10 days. He insisted that we stay all the time while we were in Istanbul, but we could not as he had relatives and other friends visiting in turn, and we didn't want to offend them, so we stayed with other friends after that. Ali Pasha took us to watch the selamdhek, the ceremonial visit of the Sultan Abdul Hamid II to the mosque every Friday. This was something we would not have seen otherwise as it was very difficult to get permission. It was a very intersting and pompous function, something as if from "1001 Nights", unforgetable. The sultan was escorted by his ladies-in-waiting, princesses (both single and married), members of the court, higher ranking officers, all the ministers, the military and civilian authorities, and the diplomatic corps.

Until the spring of 1904, we were a happy family, had a normal life, and were all very busy. Mother and sister were engaged inside the house, and with social entertaining, ladies charity committees and councils. Kel, as the representative of the Malcijas of Shkreli was engaged with authorities. Gasper was engaged with the estate and business affairs. To me, they left the administration, book-keeping, correspondence and management of our factory in Shkodër.

In March 1904, Gasper returned from Istanbul in poor health. Kel and Ninja (our sister) went with Gasper to Trieste to see the doctors and find out what was the matter with him. They did not find anything wrong, and presumed that a change of the air would do him good. So, they returned via Venice, Rome & Napoli to Shkodër. But, it did not help. On the 23rd of April 1904, he died, opening a deep wound in our hearts. This unexpected death came to us like lightning out of a blue sky. His life was ended in the spring of life. Besides family and friends, the bajraktar and the eminent people of the Shkreli provinces, delegates of both Malcijas, the authorities and the eminent people of Shkodër, Catholics as well as Muslims, came to pay him last respects.

As if it wasn't enough, about seven months later, Ninja died of a heart attack. Since Gasper's death, she had not felt well. Now her passing away left us with more grief. We were unconsolable and were also afraid for mother. Her heart was not very strong and these two deaths made matters worse. To my regret, to prevent our mother from coming across them and the painful memories they might trigger, we gave away a trunk full of the folk songs Ninja had collected to somebody, and I don't recall now whom. Back then, I didn't know the value of this rich collection of works. Hopefully, someone has made use of her hard and patient work. Ninja had a funeral like Gasper's. People wanted to show how much they empathized with us.

Kel met Ali Pasha for the last time in 1905 in Istanbul and told him about Gasper's and Ninja's deaths. This information deeply distressed Ali and his family. They immediately sent an affectionate telegram to mother and me in Shkodër. Hanmi [Hanuma-hanmi is the Turkish title of a wife of a high ranking official, equivalent to "Lady" or "Madame"] wished she was near our mother so they could mourn together, as recently they had lost their elder son, Saladin Bey, who drowned. As long as Kel

43

was in Instanbul, they insisted he stay with them, which Kel did to comfort Ali and Hanmi.

At that time in Istanbul, there were many Kurdistan soldiers and noblemen of the clan, among them, Ali Pasha's brother. To protect one Kurd family, both brothers came into conflict with the Governor General. The hostility became serious, ended up with armed fighting and the Governor was shot. The members of the Governor's party got furious and did their best to persuade the sultan that Ali Pasha and his brother, with their large familiies, soldiers and noblemen from Kurdistan, posed a danger to Istanbul and the sultan himself.

Sultan Abdul Hamid II, who lived in fear that someone was going to kill him, signed the decree that Ali Pasha and his family were to be sent to Tripoli [Tarabulluzë, Lybia]. The decree also included: brothers, sisters, in-laws, attendants and servants - all in all about three thousand people. The Kurdish noblemen and soldiers were scattered to several places in the Ottoman Empire. There were attempts at intervention from the ambassadors of England, France, Russia and Italy, but to no avail. Ali Pasha had a very bad time in Tripoli. He rebelled against the Turks, was jailed, tortured, and died. His son Kadri Bey fought with the enemies of the sultan, and we last heard about him in 1908. During WWI, the Kurds joined England and Russia's side, against the Turks.

Shkodër's pazar [outdoor bazaar], 1905 [M1]

Chapter 4: New Families

Our dear mother Leze died of a heart attack in 1906. Although she was nearly 70, which at that time was very old age, her death was still an immense source of distress. Time passed for us without our beloveds. That year, my brother Kel married Pina [Josephine], daughter of Tukë Zadrima and Drande [Rose, maiden name Muzhani], both parents from good families. Pina's father had died when she was a child, leaving four daughters and three sons. Their mother, in order to bring them up, had to sell a large part of their property, so Pina did not bring any dowry. Kel and Pina had two children, Ndoci [Ndocë / Ndoc / Anton / Anthony] and Zana [Rosana / Rosa / Rozana]. Their other children all died in childhood.

Pina and Kel [M1]

On the 8th of September in 1908, I married Nine [Nina / Ninja / Antonia], daughter of Gasper Serreqi and Rose (daughter of Pjeter Kraja), also both from good families. The Serreqi family had a high social standing in Shkodër. From this family came Monsignor Jak [Jakë / Jaccobus / Jacob / Giacomo] Serreqi, my wife's uncle. Shuk Serreqi, also Nine's uncle, was for a time the Vali-Pasha of Shkodër.

Nine and Nush [FAM]

Pina and Nine, 1909 [FA]

The Archbishop of Albania, Monsignor Pashko Guerini, was a foreigner like nearly all bishops and archbishops in Albania had been. During his stay though, the Ottoman Authorities issued a decree that all archbishops in Albania had to be Albanian. So in 1910, Monsignor Guerini was replaced with Jak Serreqi, a well known man not only in Albania, but also in Rome. He was appointed not only as the Archbishop of Shkodër, but the first Albanian Roman Catholic Archbishop of all of Albania, even before the liberation of Albania from the Turks.

Although our families were related by marriage, we had very different political opinions. The Serreqis were members of the Autro-Clerical party, until after World War I, when Italy became the protector of the Roman Catholic Church in Albania, and they joined the Italo-Clerical party instead. When Ahmet Zog [Zogolli / Zogu / Zogë] became the King of Albania, my wife's first cousin, Zef (son of Shuk Serreqi), became his adjutant. At that time, Zef was one of the youngest generals in Europe.

To my regret, many family documents were lost in 1911, after the Malcorë revolt. The Turks took severe retaliatory steps against it, starting with Catholic families, arresting them and looking for any documents or newspapers in Albanian language (which were deemed illegal), or writing concerning Albania's liberation from the Turks. Although we didn't have anything legitimately compromising, we had to burn many documents with which I had hoped to one day write about our family. We were related to the Bajraktar of Shkreli, so our family was deemed a target. We had many documents in Albanian that concerned the tribe and our family. With a heavy heart, I watched the flames destroy all of them... three large trunks worth, gone. There was no choice. Either we destroy the documents ourselves, or get arrested, exiled to Minor Asia and have the Ottoman authorities destroy the documents anyway.

Monsignor Jak Serreqi [M1]   Zef Serreqi, 1933 [M1]

In turns, Kel and I travelled to the east or to Western Europe, sometimes alone, sometimes with our wives. After my wedding, we went abroad to Dubrovnik [Ragusa] with our wives, Pina and Nine. Before going, we made them change from their national costumes (which were also really beautiful and expensive) to the dresses that were worn at the time in Western Europe. The national costumes nowadays are only worn when they go to weddings, important parties or special festivities. Kel and I were the first in Shkodër, of either Catholics or Muslims, to make our wives go out unveiled and dressed in Western European clothes. Our family, as well as the families of our wives were against this, and what was more astonishing was that the Catholic Church was too. But, we did not listen to them as we wanted our wives to take their place with us as equals. For this, we made many enemies in Shkodër among the orthodox who opposed modern ideas.

Nine and I would soon have three daughters, Zina [Lesina / Lexe / Teresa / Ziny], Gita [Margerita] and Zela [Gisela / Gisela / Giselle / Gysela], and a son Joseph. We also lost five children in childhood. Every time Kel or I chose the name Mati or Gasper for our sons, they died. For Kel and my weddings, as well as each time our children were born, there were festivities and banquets. As time went on, our house was full with children, cheerful and merry.

Top: Kel & Nush; Bottom: Pina, Zina and Nine [FAM]

In 1911, I was in Istanbul alone as Kel had to return to Shkodër for urgent business. After I saw to all my business, I started to pay visits to friends and relatives. Lastly, I went to see Ruzdhi Pasha. There, the Hanmi informed me that Madame Berta (Vasa) was in Istanbul (for a time, she and her sons had houses in both Beirut and Istanbul). The Hanmi persuaded me to go visit with her.

They were right to say that Madame Berta was a beauty. She really was, despite her age, a real lady. She received me cordially, shaking hands and smiling. In French she said, "Enfin" (meaning at last). I uttered some poor excuses justifying that when we came to Istabul she was always in Beirut. She replied with gentleness and comprehension, saying that she did not blame us, the younger generation, and continued that she was happy to hear that the sons of Leze were doing so well. Her sons had always told her how kind and affectionate Leze was towards them and what a wonderful lady she was. We had a long heart-to-heart talk about our families. At that time, her sons were in Beirut, but she suggested that I should go and see them as we were friends.

I followed her advice, and took the next boat to Beirut. I stayed with them three weeks, had a wonderful time, met and saw many marvelous people, places and things. We were constantly invited to banquets and festivities. This for me was the first and last visit to Beirut. From Beirut, I returned to Istanbul, where Madame Berta insisted that I stay with her. I stayed two more weeks, before returning to Shkodër. I promised Madame Berta that the next time we came to Istanbul, we would come directly to her house. To my regret though, historical events precluded the fullfillment of our wishes and that promise as it was the last time I visited Istanbul as well. In 1912, the Balkanik wars started, and in 1913, the Turkish army was defeated and departed from Shkodër, cutting Albania off from Istanbul. Then in 1914, World War I started. After that, we never saw our relatives in Istanbul again.

Kel and Nush [FAM]

In the spring of 1912, we got some packages from Vienna. When our two employees, Kola and Gasper, went to fetch them, the customs officer refused to hand them over. Kel went to intervene, but without success because the officer required additional documentation. Kel tried to explain to him that the documents he already presented were sufficient, as had been in the past, but it was useless. It was clear to us that the documents weren't the problem, but that someone wanted to try to harm us. To provide all the documents he asked for would have taken a long time, but we had not choice so Kel and I went to the Austrian Consul in Shkodër and asked him if he could help us in obtaining the documents faster.

The consul saw immediately that the documents we had were sufficient and told us to leave this case in his hands. After we left, he sent his cavass [kafaz, an official attendant in all consulates in the Ottoman Empire, who escorted the consul on official business] to fetch the packages, but he too got the same answer from the customs officer. That infuriated the consul, so he ordered his carriage and went to the Pasha of Shkodër with his cavass, as the consul considered this an affront against Austria.

The pasha was surprised by the consul's unannounced visit, and when he heard the reason he promised to resolve the case. The consul said with firmness, "I want these packages of Shkreli's now, or I am pulling the Austrian flag down in the consulate". Pulling down a flag in a consulate meant severing diplomatic relations with that country. The pasha, seeing that the consul was very agitated, although not understanding why, gave the order for the customs officer to release the packages and have them delivered immediately to where the consul was waiting.
We, at home and in the office, had no idea what a commotion had been caused over our packages. A short time later, to our great surprise, the consul arrived in his carriage, with his cavass and behind them three men carrying our packages. He had come in person to show Austrian influence. All of Shkodër was astonished. The customs officer also came, to beg pardon and implore us not to prosecute him, as he, in reality, had thought those documents necessary. He informed us that the authorities wanted to take steps against him, as they wanted to know who was behind it all. He maintained that this was his deed alone (it would have been worse for him had he revealed the truth).

The pasha invited Kel to come to see him. Kel went and the pasha asked him, "For God's sake, Mikel Effendi, why did you not come directly to me?". Kel answered that we did not imagine that those steps would be taken, and so much fuss created. After this was explained, Kel asked the pasha to pardon the customs officer this one time, as he was young and had just made a mistake. The pasha was very angry with this employee and wanted to punish him severely, but after Kel's pleading, he consented as a favour to Kel, to only transfer him from this priviledged job to a less important one.

When the revolutions to free Albania started, our house was tumultuous. As representatives of the Malcija Shkreli, we had people coming and going with news to and from the Malcijas all the time. The Montenegrins, with the aid of the Serbians [Serben], surrounded Shkodër from September 1912 until the 23 of April 1913 when they entered Shkodër. That siege did huge damage to Shkodër and especially the poor people who, because of food shortages, suffered hunger and distress. All the rich houses organized committees to collect and distribute food, medicines, etc., to those in need as there were people who were already starving. The Montenegrins stayed a month, then left as they were ordered by the Great Powers to get out.

Austria, supported by Italy and Germany, made a firm demand that Shkodër remain part of Albania. Russia and France, on the other hand, insisted that it be given to Montenegro. To prevent war in Europe, England intervened and it was decided that Shkodër would come under an international occupation. So, Shkodër was occupied by the armies of England, France, Germany, Austro-Hungary, and Italy, with Russia represented by France. It was the time of "Internationality" in Shkodër, as we used to say. Although our family did not belong to the Austrian Party, we were in good relations with the Consulate of Austria in Shkodër. I can only say good things about the consul and the members of the Austrian Consulate.

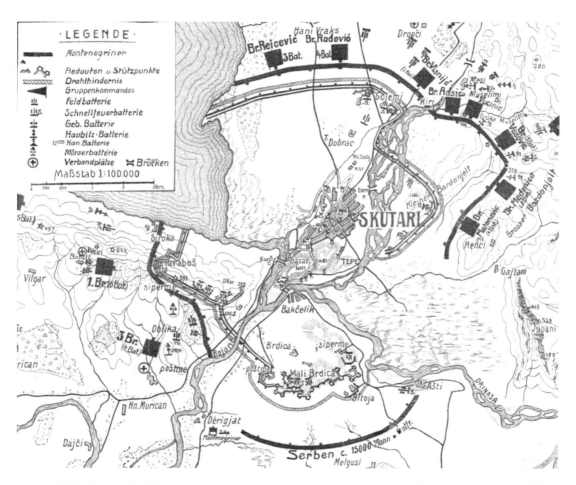

1912 Shkodër [Skutari] surrounded by Montenegrin and Serbian forces [PD]

Our family wished and believed in a free Albania, comprising all Albanians, without interference from other powers. We believed in a strong Balkan, all the Balkan nations joined in a league and confederation. "Balkan to the Balkans" was our policy and motto, as well as that of Essad Pasha Toptani.

Chapter 5: World War I

In 1914, World War I started. Austria and Germany left Albania, but the other allies remained. By 1915, Albania still hadn't significantly felt the war yet. There were shortages, but not affecting important articles. Then in 1916, the horrors swept all across Europe. The Central Powers consisted of: Austria, Hungary, Germany, Turkey and later Bulgaria. The Triple Entente consisted of: Russia, France, Great Britain and their allies: Japan, Italy, Portugal, Belgium, Serbia, Montenegro, Romania [Rumania], and the U.S.A..

It was already a year and five months into the war. Success had been on the side of the Central Powers. Serbia was defeated and had to retreat through Albania and Montenegro, to cross the Adriatic Sea and reach the Allies [The Great Retreat]. For the Serbian army, this was a disaster. They entered Albania in poor condition, exhausted, starving and on their last legs because of typhus and other diseases. Many of them collapsed and died on the way. They had to reach Shëngjin in the Lesh [Lezhë] district on the Adriatic Sea. The Serbian Command arrived in Shkodër with Regent Alexander. The streets were covered with retreating Serbian soldiers. The Austrian army was attacking the mountain Lovćen [Lovdschen], near Kotor [Cattaro, Montenegro]. It was the most important strategic summit in Montenegro, so the Austrian battleships anchored in Tivar [Antivari on the Adriatic Sea, near Lake Shkodër] to bombard it.

Map from Boka Kotorska, 1913.

Shkodër was unable to feed all the refugees and the retreating Serbian army. The houses of Muslims, Catholics and Orthodox alike were crowded with refugees, as were the schools and garrisons. Some of the families accepted the refugees voluntarily,

some didn't but they had to according to the orders of the special commission created to accommodate these unfortunate people. We, among those on the side of the Allies, felt sorry for the refugees. Those favoring the Central Powers were happy that Austria was winning.

Troops retreating through Shkodër, 1916 [PD]

Serbs being evacuated to boats at Durrës [Durazzo], 1916 [PD]

Into our home, we invited: the Serbian Finance Minister, Dr. Momčilo Ninčić, his father-in-law, Rasha Milošević, a minister and his daughter Radmila (after the war, she married the minister Branko Lazarević). For the Regent Alexander, who was in a hotel in Shkodër, we sent all he needed from A-Z for his room from our home. When our first guests left, we invited Dr. Nikola Vučetić, his wife, Dr. Maria Vučetić-Prita, their daughter Dušica, and the two nephews of his wife. All our guest were from Belgrade [Beograd].

Dr. Momčilo
Ninčić [PD]

Regent Alexander
(King of Yugoslavia) [PD]

Serbian King Peter I, as he was not on good terms with his father-in-law King Nikola of Montenegro, did not want to retreat through Montenegro so instead he went through East Albania, Zadrimë and Lesh, where Essad Pasha Toptani was in power. After the Serbian command left Albania, King Nikola of Montenegro arrived with his family and escorts, and retreated through Albania to Shëngjin. A warship awaited them there, sent by Italian King Vittorio Emmanuele [Victor Emmanuel III], his father-in-law (as Nikola had married his daughter, Helena).

King Peter
of Serbia
retreating
to the
mountains
of Albania
[S]

Austria had occupied Montenegro and was marching to Shkodër. For our family and political party, the approaching army was a huge threat. The Consul of France in Shkodër, monsieur Billecocque, sent his secretary to our house with a message that Kel and I should get ready in a hurry to leave Albania immediately. He had reserved two places for us on the destroyer that was coming to get the consul, the military personnel and employees.

We could have left our wives and children behind, as they would have been well off financially and with household staff and servants to take care of them, and with Kolë [Kol / Nikola] Paldeda as the supervisor. The families of both wives, Pina and Nine, were aligned with the Austrian Political Party, and my wife's uncle was the Roman Catholic Archbishop so they would have all been protected.

Kel could not make up his mind, saying that we were not guilty of anything, in fact the opposite - we had helped so many people, why should we leave. Pina, Nine and I tried to persuade him that it would be better to go with the Allies and be free, than stay here and get caught by the Austrians. Pina and Nine said that they would be worried for us if we stayed. It was all useless though, as Kel was an optimist and finally suggested that I go without him. Of course, he knew that I would never do that, especially as he wasn't feeling well. I replied, "It is kismet, I am staying too" [kismet means fate].

Besides the French Consul, the Italian Consul in Shkodër (Signor De Francendis, a great politician and man) also sent his secretary to tell us to get ready to leave Albania. He had also reserved for us two places on a steamship on which he and his personnel would leave Albania. Not even this invitation changed Kel's mind. So we brothers remained in Shkodër, and faced the Austro-Hungarian occupation of Albania. This was a bad turn of events for us and our families.

The avantgarde of the Austrian army were nearing the river Buna, near Shkodër, and started to climb Tarabosh, the mountain overlooking Shkodër. The last of the Serbian soldiers had just crossed Baçadhek Bridge, the way out of Shkodër. The Mayor of Shkodër, Muharem Bey Gjylbeg Gramshi, sent word that the eminents of the district, merchants, wealthy people, and the representatives of the Mulsim, Catholic and Othodox religions should assemble in the town hall to welcome the commandant of the Austro-Hungarian army. People crowded the streets to watch.

Shkodër's mayor, Muharem Gjylbegaj, had been in service of the Ottoman Empire for a long time. In 1913, he had greeted the Montenegrins, and after six weeks, the International Missions. In 1914-1915, he collaborated with the reactionista. In 1915 he dealt with the Montenegrins retreating through the country, and now in 1916, he welcomed the Austo-Hungarian army. He did not remain in the position to see them leave though. That privilege fell on Musa Juka.

The mayor gave a welcome speech in Albanian, which Kolë Kodheli (the town hall's secretary) translated into German. The commandant of the Austro-Hungarian army thanked them for the magnificent reception, promising that the army had not come as an enemy, but as a friend of Albania. We, in support of the Allied Party, did not participate in the welcome ceremony. We were never government employees, but were always independent. It would have been hipocrisy on our part to participate, as everyone knew which side we were on. On the other hand, we did no harm to the Austrian army, we minded our own business.

The moment the Austro-Hungarian army assumed power in Shkodër, they posted their officers in all the offices, temporarily. In the town hall, they put Hauptman Tash, an overly-stern Hungarian man. At the first meeting of the Municipal Council, there was a long and rigorous debate of whom to intern, as countries often do in times of war. They finalized on: Alush Lohja [Alush agë Lohje / Luhje / Luhe], Malo Bey Bushati, Mikel Shkreli (my brother, Kel), Hasan Bey Bushati, Nikola [Kola] Berović, Rexhep Yella, Simon Gjon Laca, Mirash [Mirashi] Luca, Brahim Bey Sokoli and some others.

Alush Lohja, 1932 [M2]

Malo Bey Bushati [M2]

Shortly before midnight on Monday the 31st of January 1916, armed guards patrolled around Shkodër while others surrounded the houses of those they wanted. Since Saturday the 29th, Kel had been ill with the flu and pneumonia. Our family doctors, Dr. Rauf [Rauf Angoni] and Dr. Basria, visited Kel often while he was ill. The news of his illness had spread, so we had a continuous flow of visitors, relatives and friends, inquiring about his health. Kel's illness was well known in Shkodër, but still on the

31st, they came to take him away. The garden was full of Austrian soldiers, and some of them entered the house.

Simon Gjon Laca [M1]

Dr. Rauf Angoni [M2]

My brother, being so weak from pneumonia, asked in a low voice if they could not wait until he recovers. The officer who led the patrol, an honest man, seeing how ill Kel was told me that he could not be of help and make that decision, but I could send somebody to the Municipal Committee. However, it was presided over by the inhumane Hauptman Tash, who didn't agree to this. He ordered Kel to be taken to the Austrian military hospital, and he didn't allow us to drive Kel there, he made him go on foot, even though he was ill.

My poor brother, Kel. We helped him get dressed, and slowly go down the stairs to the garden full of soldiers. The officer (God bless him) gave permission to me, Kolë Paldeda and some of our manservants to help Kel and to accompany him to the hospital. The children were all asleep, and did not hear what was happening. Pina, Nine and the staff were crying and in despair parting with Kel.

While helping him to the hospital, he told me how sorry he was for not having listened to me and leaving when it was possible, and giving the family more worries. He hoped that they would leave me alone. My brother did not know that soon they would imprison me too. The officer who came for Kel asked for a doctor. The doctor was Hungarian too. He examined Kel and established that he was not so bad that he could not be interned with the others the following day. What a ruthless, inhuman being, worse than Hauptman Tash. He ordered that we leave, so heartbroken, we did and promised to return the next day.

Early in the morning, Kolë went to inquire about Kel, but they did not let him approach the hospital. We sent word to Palokë [Palok / Paloka] Zadrima (Pina's brother), Lec (Nine's brother), and Shuk (Nine's uncle). Shuk, Palokë, Lec, Baba Gasper ["baba" as he was Nine's father, and our children's grandfather] and many relatives immediately came after hearing about Kel. Baba Gasper told us that they had taken Simon Laca too, the husband of her cousin, Adusha [Dusha Laca, daughter of Filip Serreqi].

Palokë Zadrima [M2]

Lec Serreqi [M2]

We tried all possible means of persuasion to get Kel to be placed in the nun's hospital. Meanwhile, Pina, Nine and I went to the hospital to see Kel but we couldn't find him. The doctor, a wicked man, had found him well enough to travel (as if someone with pneumonia should). When we asked where he had been taken, they did not know. I, Kolë and two of our manservants went all around town in search of Kel. I wanted to give him at least a few hundred Napoleons (gold money, the currency of the day), as he had to leave without it the night before.

Gita Shkreli & Adusha Laca, 1921 [M1]   Filip Serreqi, 1923 [M2]

We finally found Kel at the pier, about to board a ship taking him across Lake Shkodër to Virpazar [Virbazar] in Montenegro. We met, gave him the money and we parted with heavy hearts. Later on, he told me how Mirash, Nikola and other friends had helped him there by supporting him under his arms, practically carrying him as he was unable to walk. They were forced to go from Viripazar to Rijeka Crnojevića [Rječka, Montenegro] on foot as an additional hardship, which in Kel's state was torture.

From there, they went to Cetinje, and then to Kotor [Cattaro] on the Adriatic Sea. Kel arrived there exhausted, and at last they put him in a hospital. We had many friends there, and they came to see him and bring whatever he needed. We repaid them double, but the favors they did for Kel could never truly be repaid. The other interned foreigners were taken through Herceg-Novi (Montenegro region on the Adriatic Sea) to the Spanjola [Spanish] and Mamula fortresses. They took Kel there too, when he got better.

Mamula Fortress [S]

Spanjola Fortress [S]

After they had sent off the first group, the authorities of Shkodër started on the second list. My name appeared among those considered. Some of the members of the council were of the opinion that I should not be interned, but others felt that I, being from the Great Malcija, could be dangerous to the Austrian army. One of the Muslims from Shkodër, Hasan Bey, son of Beilo Bey (a friend of the family), stood in my defence with these words: "It is a shame to behave like this gentlemen, and exhibit a weakness as if Shkodër is afraid of the Shkrelis". After those words, the others had no courage to insist upon it and, for the time being, let it go.

From the moment they took Kel, I had no peace as I was sure that it wouldn't be long before they came for me. I started to settle the affairs of our estate, business, money, gold, jewels and other precious items. To save as much of it as possible, I gave as many items as I could to Baba Gasper and relatives of Nine and Pina: Shuk &

Monsignor Serreqi and Palokë. They all belonged to the Austrian Party (were Austrophiles) so should not be disturbed by the Austrians. So when the Austrians came for me too, our family's wealth was well protected. Only Kolë knew of these activities.

In the early morning on the day after Kel was taken, an Austrian armed patrol with two policemen came to our house. Using the pretense of looking for Mirash Luca, whom they claimed they'd been told was hiding at our house, they searched the premises. They looked all around the house and found nothing, then continued to look outside, and in wardrobes, cupboards, bookcases and closets. Nine became exasperated and could not bear it any longer. "Mirash is not a foolish man to come and hide in our house, and also he is not a needle, able to hide himself among the linen", she said. The policemen felt shame as they were from Shkodër, and knew that she was a daughter of the Serreqis', so they left.

On the Friday after they interned Kel, Dr. Salem, dressed in an Austrian officer uniform, came to our house and arrogantly started to shout, "Where did you take my furniture when you emptied the house for the Serbian and Montenegro officers". Dr. Salem was an arrogant man from Split (or nearby), who later worked in Shkodër and turned out to be an Austrian sympathiser. When Austria declared war in 1914, he closed the home he was staying at (only the furniture was his), and went to Austrian occupied territory. He returned with the Austro-Hungarian army.

He continued, "Though I found the furniture, there are other things missing and I want them from you". I responded, "We have not taken anything. Muharem Bey, who is still the president of the Municipality, was then the chairman of the committee which was requisitioning unoccupied houses and making them available for the retreating Serbian and Montenegro army. Your furniture was taken to a safe place, an inventory list was made, and the documents were signed, first by Muharem Bey, and then, among other signatories, was Mr. Kel Çoba, who is here with you". He was the owner of Kel's house, as well as Dr. Salem's. I continued, "Go and look for the missing items at the place where your furniture and other things were originally stored". He responded, "You will see what I will do to you. Today, Austria is in power". I knew that he would try to harm me with his lies, on top of everything else, as he was holding a grudge that we never engaged him as our family doctor.

Kel Çoba, 1924 [M2]

After he left, Pina, Nine, the children and I mostly stayed home. The house was still full of relatives and friends who were not afraid to be in a household from which a member was interned by the Austrian authorities. I stopped our children's daily excursion in the carriages, the garden around the house was big enough for them. I suggested my wife visit her uncle, the archbishop, and relay Dr. Salem's accusations and peronal threats.

Kel Shkreli's carriage [M1]

Nine and two manservants proceeded in our carriage to her Uncle Jak. The reception room of the archdiocese was overcrowded that day, due to the arrival of Archduke Franz Salvator, the nephew of the Austro-Hungarian Emperor, Franz Josef. Nine's arrival was announced to the archbishop, as she urgently wanted to see him. He asked that she be ushered in, even though he was with the archduke at the time. Introductions were made and the archbishop laughed, mentioning to the archduke that his niece was married to the opposing political side.

Painting of Archduke Franz Salvator, 1905 [PD]

After a short conversation (all three of them spoke Italian), the archduke withdrew to the suites to receive an audience. When they were alone, Nine told her uncle all that had happened with Dr. Salem. Uncle Jak said that he would immediately ask Dr. Salem to come settle it. At the same time, he reproached me and Kel, as he had many times warned us not to expose ourselves. Back then we were fortunate to not need anyone's help, well-to-do and independent, but look at us now. Nine answered that we were still involved in this way of political life when we were occupied by the Ottoman Empire. He laughed, and told her that he understood what she was saying, that their interventions during that time had immensely helped the people and the church, and that she had learned a lot from the Shkrelis.

When Nine returned home, she was pretty upset. She told me that since we brothers were active in politics and intervening on other people's behalf for justice and welfare, we should not have stayed until the Austrian occupation and put ourselves in this situation. I agreed with her. It seems this was our fate since we could not talk Kel into leaving. Thank God we were well off and did not have to depend on others.

The Austro-Hungarian army started to come continually, and take things that they required from our house and warehouses, and issue receipts for them. The days passed. Visits from friends and relatives grew rare and short as everybody was frightened for themselves. Even Palokë, Pina's brother, stopped coming for the same reason. I had nobody to ask for advice, all the responsibility was on my shoulders, and I was not feeling well. I was exasperated.

On Monday evening, the 17th of February 1916, I did not feel like eating and told Nine and Pina that I just wanted to take a bath and go to bed as I was feeling unwell. The children and female servants, including Age, the most senior female servant who looked after our son Gasper, had already eaten and withdrawn to their rooms. Menservants were preparing for their dinner. Before Nine retired for the night, she came to see how I was.

I was half asleep, but I heard Nine whisper to Pina, "I am afraid that tonight they are coming for Nush too, as for a while now, I have been hearing heavy steps of soldiers surrounding our house just the same as it was when they came for Kel". Pina answered, "Stop your foreboding prediction so that harm will not come". With that, they both went to bed and were soon asleep.

I remained awake. Towards midnight, I heard the banging at the main gate's knocker. I cried out to wake Nine and Age, and at that moment, there was a knock on our bedroom door. The manservant who was on guard duty (since the Austrian occupation, our manservants took turns on guard duty at night) informed me that the Austrian soldiers had surrounded the outside wall of the gardens and wanted to enter. I told him to open the gate.

As soon as he opened the gate, the soldiers rushed in, surrounded the house. Some of them along with the leading officer entered the house and filled the hall. Age wanted to go and wake Pina and Kolë, but they wouldn't let her move. The heavy steps of the soldiers had awakened other manservants, and one of them went to wake up Kolë, whose room was in the other wing of the house. The other manservants were surrounded and not allowed to move. One of them had to show the officers which was my bedroom. The officer entered it with two officials from the police.

The officer told me in Italian (as he was from Istria, and had been told that I spoke Italian), "Mister Shkreli, before we search the whole house, please surrender your arms and ammunition". I answered, "Mister officer, all the arms and ammunition have already been handed over, and we have receipts for the same. There are no further arms or ammunition in our possession". The officer, not believing what I said, said that it would be better if I handed them over peacefully. I was sure there were none in the house so I said, "Please conduct a thorough search. I am prepared to take on the consequences".

After they conducted a thorough search or every room, storage space, and crevice in the house, he realized that the accusations were false, and with an uncomfortable look on his face, said, "In the name of the law, raise your hands", at which point I was frisked, "and please get ready as you will have to come with me". The officer then sent away the two officers that accompanied him and turned toward the door. For a moment, he stopped, turned to me and whispered, "Mister Shkreli, please take with you everything you might need and that you can carry, as they will remove you from Shkodër". He didn't need or have time to step out as I had nothing to hide, and all my personal things were already packed. I had been anticipating these events ever since Kel and many others in the Malcijas had been taken.

This officer was a decent human being, and I'll never forget his words in this difficult time for me and my family, "According to the accusers, I thought I was coming for a well-armed mighty barbarian, while instead I found a real gentleman". Pina, hearing all the commotion of searching our rooms, wanted to join us but the soldiers barred her exit. I requested from the officer that he kindly allow me to say goodbye to my children and my sister-in-law (Pina), as my wife was already beside me. He issued the order and Pina brought by daughter Zina, and two female servants came with Gita and nephew (Ndoci), as well as my daughter (Zela) and niece (Zana) in cradles.

It was a very touching moment which I can never forget, and which is always foremost on my mind. Nine, Pina, and the children were crying. Gita was struggling to reach me, and Zela and Zana, now awake in their cradles, were also crying. God gave me fortitude when I took leave of my family, embracing Nine, my childen, Pina, my niece and nephew. I shook hands with all the servants, male and female, then turned to Nine and Pina and told them, "Bear this with courage. Look after the children, house, estate, etc. as this is our present fate". Age said in a quiet voice, "Master Nush, internment is for brave men, not women. Don't worry, we will endure all together. The important thing is that your return to us in good health".

The officer addressed my family saying not to worry as nothing was going to happen to me, this was temporary and that I would soon be back amongst them. Before leaving the house, I entered the hall, saw a large crowd of soldiers and had to smile. I said to the officer, "It seems absurd to me that you have gone through so much trouble and brought all these soldiers when one soldier would have been enough to come for me". He replied, "I must admit that I was surprised when I saw that I was dealing with a gentleman, but the report we had was that the household was well manned, armed and ready to fight back and that was the reason for bringing all these soldiers".

I asked him to allow Kolë to escort me to the boat, which he agreed to. At the pier, I took leave from Kolë and entrusted my family and estate to his care. We had complete confidence in him as he had stood by us through these difficult and unpredictable times. When I boarded the ship, I found myself among the cream of Shkodër's society. Although it was night and dark, I recognized the voices of Riza Bey Kopliku, Myrto Llazani and Beqir Neziri. Ali Bey Kolona [Kolonja] approached and greeted me, and then I noticed Him Kastrati and Kolë Ashiku were also there. Beqir Neziri was angry that they had come to take us during the night, and frightened our wives and children, as if they were so aftaid of us that they could not have come for us during the daytime.

Riza Bey Kopliku [M2]

Beqir Neziri [M2]

They said they were surprised to see me too, knowing that I was the son-in-law of the Serreqi family, who had always belonged to the Austrian party. I agreed, but replied that Kel and I, as they knew, had always been aligned with the opposition's party. All of us on the ship belonged to Essad Pasha's Party. It was a very cold and windy night, and we were on the open deck until the morning. The officer on duty invited us to come in as he had to take down our names, professions, etc. Seeing what kind of people we all were, he became more courteous and apologized for not having seen us during the night when we arrived, but he had been too tired and had fallen asleep. He said, "From now on, you are free to use the salon and go around the ship. I see that you are gentlemen and that you will not try to escape and cause trouble". Riza Bey, as the oldest, replied, "Mister Captain, when an Albanian gives his word, he never breaks it and we thank you for your kind greetings". When we disembarked, we had to go through the same things as Kel and his fellow companions had experienced. It was torture. If the guards were humane, they would have let us buy food with our own money. The guards were sadistic though, and the food they gave us wasn't fit to be eaten.

Kel, I and others spent over a year in the fortresses, Mamula and Spanjola, at the Boka of Kotor [Bocche di Cattaro, the mouth of the Bay of Kotor]. Contrary to international laws, instead of keeping us as political internees should have, they imprisoned us like criminals. In Shkodër, the Austro-Hungarian army requisitioned everything from our warehouses, which had once been full of goods from the family's import / export business, including wool and bristles from our livestock. They also took from the house: all the dishes, pots and pans, bowls, mattresses, quilts, pillows, furniture, and whatever was made of copper. They took as much as they could, and only left some receipts.

After we were interned, they also requisitioned to use part of our house for their officers. According to Albanian law, when the male head of the house is not present, no strange men are allowed to stay inside. My wife, Nine, confronted the official who had brought the officers about the law. The official protested, but Nine said that if he was not familiar with the laws, she would get an intervention from those who did. Then she gave the order for the gate to be closed, and nobody admitted, as she felt strong, being born a Serreqi. She got ready and went in our carriage with Kolë to the archiocese, to see her Uncle Jak. She informed him of the problem. He settled the problem by allowing only officers with wives to be in the requisitioned wing. The house was large, and had separate entrances, so they'd never need to have any contact with the other occupants.

The Austro-Hungarian authorities in Shkodër, supposedly to be kind, advised Pina and Nine to submit to them a petition to set free their husbands. When Pina and Nine presented the request, the authorities returned it with the excuse that it was not done correctly. They wanted the petition modified so that Pina and Nine request amnesty for their husbands. Our wives replied that they had no reason to ask for amnesty, as their husbands had done nothing wrong, and there was therefore no grounds to request amnesty.

Our relatives and many friends tried to persuade Pina and Nine to rewrite the petition as the Austro-Hungarian authorities wanted, but our wives were resolute in their decision. Had they made the change, it would have been an admission of guilt, whereas there had been no wrongdoing on our part. When Kel and I came back and learned about this, we were proud and in agreement with their resolute stand. After more than a year, all those of us who were interned were brought in front of the Military Court of Justice. The judges realized that we had all done nothing against the Austro-Hungarian army and sent us home.

In 1917, Kel and I came back to Shkodër. My poor little son Gasper had already died. Thank God all the others were well, as when we were interned, we seldom heard news from home. Although we all came back, many returned with poor health. My brother Kel returned home with his lungs destroyed, and no wonder. He was taken from his home with pneumonia and left since then in the depths of a fortress where little light and no sunlight reached. He now got the best medical care and food, and improved, but was always delicate and needed care after that.

We found our estate destroyed, the warehouses emptied, and 90% of the livestock taken by the Austro-Hungarian army. Whatever goods the army needed, they requisitioned and for all these requisitions, they left us war bonds worth 60,000 Austrian crowns (equivalent to golden Francs), one third of the real value of the goods. Kel had to be spared from worry, as he was still recovering. I too did not feel well after the time spent in that fortress, but had to set aside my personal difficulties, as all the responsibility of the family was now on me. As our family was independent and self-sufficient, we distanced ourselves from everyone and everything, and minded our own business.

Chapter 6: Albanian Independence

Before World War I, there were two Austrian Consuls in Shkodër, Consul August Ritter von Kral and Consul Hall. Although we were not friends, we were not enemies either. Once Kel and I got into a heated discussion with Consul Kral about the political situation in Europe. Consul Kral said, "We are not friends, but I have great respect for you, being gentlemen of great character and personal independence, but that will be your undoing, and I feel sorry for your families". This prophecy turned into a reality.

When we came back from internment, these two consuls were still in Shkodër. The wing in our house that was requisitioned by the army was occupied by an Austrian officer's family who had been friends with Consul Kral. They visited with each other very often, especially Mrs. Kral with her children. Our garden was large and their children used to play with our children in it. After World War I, I visited Vienna and went to pay a visit to the widowed Mrs. Kral. She told me that she had written her memoirs, and where she'd written of the time in Shkodër, she also wrote about our family, those visits to our house, and how the children played together. Well, enemy or not, a gentleman is always a gentleman.

Gita & Ndoci, 1919 [FAM]

In 1918, World War I ended, the Austro-Hungarian army left Shkodër, and the Allied army arrived. Shkodër was under the command of the French and the English armies. We loaned the wing of our house that was previously occupied by the Austrian army to the French Colonel de Rodaun, a real gentleman. We became friends with his family. In 1919, when Kel was feeling better and travelled to Paris, he visited with them.

Kel and I had no intention to involve ourselves in politics, and wanted to return to taking care of our house and our interests. After the war, we started our business again, and even enlarged it with partnerships in Shkodër and Dubrovnik. Kel went to Vienna to see the doctors and check up on his health, and he took my daughter Zina with him. There he was examined by the well known professor Dr. Ortner, who had been the physician of the Haubsburg's court, as well as by Dr. Neuman and Dr. Sacks. Per their advice, he spent two months in Semmering, near Vienna, a well-known woodland resort. After that, they returned home.

Zina, 1919 [M1]

Although we were not going to get involved in politics again, that wish didn't go to plan. After Kel returned, he had to go with the other Albanian delegates to the Paris Peace Conference, and so, we again got involved in politics and exposed ourselves to scrutiny and plotting. In Paris, Kel met up with Essad Pasha Toptani. Although Albania had won liberty from Turkey and hoisted the Albanian flag in 1912, it was now a struggle to reaffirm Albania's indepedence. The conference delegates wanted to divide Albania between Greece and Yugoslavia. The Albanian Christian immigrants (as the Muslims rarely emigrated) from America, Italy and Romania as well as Albania, sent delegates to the conference to demand the recognition of Albanian independence. After a two month stay, Kel returned to Shkodër.

I had to go on business to Vienna. When I returned, Kel went to Paris again, where he met Nikola Pašić, Yugoslav's Prime Minister. When he returned, Shkodër was in turmoil, as many political parties had sprung up. Other nations wanted to play a political role to gain influence over Albania. To avoid any involvement, Kel and I went to Vienna, Kel to see the doctors, and I on business. We stayed there three months.

Prime Minister Nikola Pašić [PD]

When we returned, Shkodër had become the centre of a political war. The government was situated in Tiranë, and included Mustafa Kruja, Bazi Cans and Ahmet Zog (as Minister of Interior). Sulco Bey and Shuk Serreqi (my wife's uncle) were temporary prefects in Shkodër. The proud Shkodër people, with their long history, did not want to be governed by people from another Albanian province. People in Shkodër wanted the seat of government to remain there, as it had been since ancient times. Even under the Turks, in the 18th and 19th century, it had an autonomous government under the rule of the Viziers of Bushatli. Shkodër had the priviledge to change governors and high administrators, and later, special priviledges, such as being exempt from enlisting their sons in the army, or payment of taxes. All the rights Shkodër had under the Turks, it seemed they would now lose.

Shkodër did not even want to come under the command of Essad Pasha, not that they did not hold him in high esteem, but they did not want to be under Durrës' rule, the then temporary residence of the provisional government of liberated Albania. The worst scenario though was if Shkodër came under Tiranë's rule, and for that reason, the people of Shkodër did not want the union.

Although Kel and I hated to be involved again in politics, we could not avoid it because of our social positions. We followed the course of politics that we thought was best for the benefit of Albania. At that time, we could speak openly as we were independent socially and financially. All the responsibilities of our house and business were on me, as I didn't want to burden Kel, so I left him only the political representation, and if that got too much, I would help him out. Although I ran the house, I often listened to his advice, even if it was against our advantage, as he was the older brother. Maybe I was wrong, as I had to bear and correct many errors, but I could not behave otherwise toward him, knowing his health situation. He meant a lot to me.

Kel went again to Paris, to deal with more problems. He met Essad Pasha again, and they had a long conversation. Before he'd left, a man named Luk [Luka] Lukaj, an Albanian from a modest family from Skopje, arrived in Shkodër. He had no means so had to work for someone else to enter politics. He came to pay us a visit and as we

70

did not know him, we were polite but didn't accept him. He had spread word around Shkodër that Essad Pasha had sent him as his assistant. When Kel inquired about this, Essad got very angry, and told Kel that Luk had been spreading lies. He didn't know the man, except that when he was in Belgrade, the Yugoslav Ministry had recommended him as someone to employ as a clerk. Essad had rejected his offer as he had no need, but promised to look into it again when he returned to Albania.

A Yugoslav delegate that Prime Minister Pašić had introduced Kel to in Paris, Mr. Nešić, came to Shkodër. While he was there, we became friends as he was of the same political opinions as Essad Pasha and I, and believed that the Balkan Peninsula belonged to Balkan nations.

When Kel returned from Paris, he often went to rest in the woodlands of our estate. In January 1920, he went with Malo Bey Bushati to obtain the permissions needed to export goods from Yugoslavia to Albania as we had a business partnership in Yugoslavia. Because of the help we gave the Serbs when they retreated through Albania in 1916, we were considered "Slavophiles".

In Albania, especially in Shkodër, the situation had reached a boiling point. The Albanian border had still not been established. The government in Tiranë, or better to say the political party of Ahmet Zog, opposed the temporary government in Durrës (1918-1920), and after the Congress of Lushnjë [Lushnja], dissolved it. It had included: Mustafa Krija, Luigj Gurakuqi, Fejzi Alizoti and others.

Fejzi Alizoti (2nd Prime Minister) [PD]

Members of the Congress of Lushnjë, 1920 [PD]

A new party and government were formed with Tiranë as the capital of Albania. These changes resulted in the arrests of many politicians, many of whom lost their employment and were interned. Politics had turned against Slavophiles. But, as Kel and I had never been employed by any government, either Albanian or other nation, but had instead always remained independent, they could not take steps against us.

As the border hadn't been established, the Yugoslav army was able to come to Shiroka [Siroka] and Tarabosh [Taraboš], near Shkodër. In Podgorica (Montenegro), the Committee of Podgorica was established. Its members included Alush Lohja and Luk Lukaj, among others. The committee wanted to seize power in Albania, with the help of Yugoslavia. Although the committee was funded by Yugoslavs, the Yugoslav army and Minister of External Affairs didn't want to take action against Albania. However, the committee was able to get enough help from Yugoslavia, some Malcorë and Montenegrins, and entered Albania. They took control over Han in the Hoti province & Kastrat province (up to Koplik), with the intention of taking Kelment and Shkrel and then to enter Shkodër.

When news of this action reached Tiranë, Prime Minister Suljman Delvina consulted with ministers and decide to send Ahmet Zog to Shkodër to punish the provokers. At the time, Shkodër was governed by Sulco Bey and Shuk Serreqi. Ahmet reassigned Sulco to Koplik, to be the commander of the volunteer units, and Shuk remained as a councilor in the prefecture of Shkodër. The Committee of Podgorica had to leave all they had taken, as the Yugoslav army leadership and most of the government were opposed to their actions. This transgression by the Committee of Podgorica had bad consequences for the friendship between Albania and Yugoslavia, and damaged Essad Pasha's politics, as well as ours. Although the Committee of Podgorica was retreating, this event wasn't over yet.

The Yugoslav minister, Ljuba Nešić, who was in Shkodër, was angry and had sent to Belgrade very negative reports about the committee. When the committee planned to attack Shkodër, they sent telegrams, in Kel and my name to lend them more importance, to Prefect Shuk Serreqi and Monsignor Jak Serreqi that read, "Surrender Shkodër without a fight for your own good as we are coming". Kel and I had gone to the Shkreli region to visit our bajraktar and to celebrate a tribal festivity but we did not stay long. It seemed that the spies of Alush Lohja did not know that were back in Shkodër three days before the telegrams were sent. Of course, Sulco Bey and the Serreqis knew that we were in Shkodër and checked with us immediately to verify that the telegrams were fake. We not only didn't have any connection with the committee, but also opposed them as we wanted friendly relations with Yugoslavia.

The 2nd of August is my name day, which I've always celebrated in a big way, ever since I was born. The 1st of August 1920 was a Sunday, and a banquet was held for the eve of my name day. There were 108 guests, including relatives, friends, authorities and eminent people of Shkodër, regardless of their party affiliations. The mood was fantastic, with great merriment accompanied by musical groups and singers. Everybody was having such a good time that the banquet, contrary to custom, lasted until dawn. It was as if fate was trying to tell me that this was the last time I would be able to have such an assembly in our house. When it was over, Kel and I felt very melancholy, and went to the garden to sit in the shade of the large mulberry tree. We had a foreboding feeling in our hearts.

Close relatives stayed over for the next day's lunch and also had dinner with us, and helped entertain numerous guests who dropped by during the day. They were offered drinks, snacks and sweets, and coffee was a must, to wish me a happy name day. Gasper Shkreli (our cousin's son) came, out of breath, and told us that he'd heard from a friend employed near Ahmet Zog's office, that Ahmet had received an accusation against Kel and I, who as Slavophiles were deemed dangerous and should be distanced from Shkodër. We were greatly surprised. In the other room were: Palokë Zadrima (Pina's brother), Lec Serreqi (Nine's brother), Monsignor Jak Serreqi, Shuk, and Filip (Nine's uncles), Monsignor Luigj Bumçi (who was a member of the Regency of the Albanian Govenment and a relative).

Zina Çurçia & Lec Serreqi [M2]   Monsignor Luigj Bumçi [M2]

There were others too, but I mention only these because we took them in the other room and told them in confidence what our cousin's son had told us. They too were greatly surprised. Monsignor Bumçi said he could not believe it as he had been with Ahmet in the morning, and told him how the last night he had been celebrating my name day and planned to return again today for dinner.

Our children were enjoying the company of their cousins and aunts and were not aware of what was being discussed. Pina and Nine tried to entertain the other guests so they would not notice anything. Kel and I decided not to surrender ourselves to

73

anyone, but instead to leave Albania. The people who we'd taken into our confidence told us to wait until the next day. After dinner, our family doctor, Dr. Rauf Angoni, who was also Ahmet's friend, came to visit. He too was surprised as the same day he had shared lunch with Ahmet, and among other things, had discussed how we brothers had protested to Lubja Nešić, the Yugoslav Minister, against the Committee of Podgorica. Dr. Rauf also pleaded with us to wait and not take any steps until he spoke again with Ahmet. He also mentioned that Mr. Eshref Frasheri and Dr. Surja Pojani, Ahmet's associates in the party Poppulore, were staying with Ahmet.

After all this advice, we calmed down, and spent the dinner and evening in pleasant conversation with our guests. After the guests left, we were still worried though, and under the circumstances, decide to take precautions. The armed guards were ordered inside the garden. Whenever we went out, four armed guards escorted us. To the menservants, we gave orders not to open the gate to anybody during the night. During the day, it would be easier to avoid a forced surrender.

The next day, Kel, Palokë and the arranged armed guards went to see Dr. Rauf Angoni. They met Mr. Eshref Frasheri and Dr. Surja Pojani who said they'd spoken with Ahmet. Ahmet had confirmed that there had been an accusation against us, but had also told them that he hadn't given any orders against the Shkrelis. While Kel & Palokë were away, Mr. Ejell [Ejëll] Shiroka and some Jesuit priests came to wish me a happy name day. After they left, some high ranking clergy of the Parochia of Shkodër also visited for the same purpose. Not long after that, we heard some shots. My heart stopped as Kel was still out. I thought that something had happended to him, that they tried to take him and he was resisting. Kolë and our armed manservants went out into the street with some of the clergy who were still visiting. Kolë returned and told me it was not against Kel but that Ejell Shiroka, who was in a blood feud with Lec [Lecë] Çoba, had been killed.

Ejëll Shiroka [M2]

Ejell had left our street (fortunately, or else this feud would have involved us too), and saw Lec Çoba and was preparing to shoot him, but Lec was quicker and shot him first. Lec and Zef Shiroka ran towards our house and gave themselves to us in "besa", and according to the customs, we had to give them protection [Besa is not only a word of honour, but also a forced committment entrusting someone to your

74

safekeeping, regardless of your own position and obligations]. As if we didn't have enough of our own troubles and worries, but now we had to hide them.

Lec Çoba [M2]

Friar Anton Harapi & Zef Shiroka [M2]

When Kel and Palokë left Dr. Rauf Angoni's place, they heard that someone had been shot near our street and returned breathless. The police arrived after them, looking for Lec and Zef, but were unable to find them. We sent Kolë to Ndoc Çoba, who was a minister in Ahmet's cabinet, and also sent word to Monsignor Bumçi, because Zef was his nephew. They all assembled in our house. Although Ejell was not shot on our property, he had just left our house so we felt some responsibility. Kel went to see Ejell's son. All those assembled in our house agreed that we did not lose face, and that we were not involved in this vendetta as Ejell was the first to draw a gun. I am describing this event to you, my children, so that you can understand the customs of those times, the courage, and the responsibilities of the family.

Mr. Çoba and Monsignor Bumçi settled the affair. Lec and Zef surrendered themselves to the authorities. With a witness to the event in court, they were set free as they acted in self-defence. But now, it was important to reconcile with Ejell's son, or else he would take on the vendetta to not lose face and the honour of his house. As we were related to both sides, our family had to be the mediator. A couple of days after the funeral, they all assembled in our house and the vendetta was settled without further bloodshed.

At that time, our business partners in Yugoslavia requested that one of us, Kel or I, come to Yugoslavia because he had not received the needed permits for exporting goods in time, goods we had already paid for. It was very important for us to go as soon as possible, or else we'd lose our significant investment. This partnership consisted of our partner supplying the work, and us financing part of it. Kel went to obtain a passport, but was given some excuses and denied one. After an intervention by our friends, who were friends with Ahmet, they gave Kel the passport but required that I stay in Shkodër. On the 15th of August, 1920, Kel left by ship on Lake Shkodër, went through Cetinje, Kotor [Cattaro] and finally arrived in Dubrovnik [Ragusa].

Dubrovnik [S]

The 16th was a melancholy day for me. Kel was safe and free in Yugoslavia, but I was kept back as a hostage in Shkodër. For even the slightest provocation or reason, I could be arrested. The internment by the Austrians during World War I was enough for me. There was still fighting with the Committee of Podgorica going on, and volunteers were continually coming from all the provinces of Albania to Shkodër. That day in the afternoon, I went out with Palokë and my armed escort to the cafe in Miletbaçe (center of Shkodër) to distract myself a little. I met Dr. Rauf Angoni there, as well as Mr. Sefije, Dr. Surja, Mr. Eshref Bey and others. I spent an hour with them, then returned home.

At home, I found pleasure playing with the children, especially Joseph, who was four months old and every day brought something new into our lives. As usual, in the evening we had guests, relatives and friends. The next morning, Baba Gasper (Nine's father) and Shan [Marc] Koleka (a cousin on my mother's side) came over. They were also at my disposal, should I need to flee to a place of safety. I was determined never to be a political internee again. Shan left, and then a message arrived from Monsignor Serreqi that Shuk was coming and that I should remain at home. Shuk arrived and explained what Ahmet had told him: when the accusations were brought up in council, Ahmet had said that if there were measures taken against Kel and I, then they should also be taken against all the political opponents, and not just some.

As soon as Shuk and Baba Gasper left, Gjon Dedë [Deda] Shkreli, the current Bajraktar of the Shkreli tribe, and Pjetër Mirashi [Marashi] came from Gruemirë [Gruda / Grudë, north of Shkodër], arrived. The bajraktar told me that coming from the Shkrel region, through Koplik, he had met Sulco Bey, the commander in chief of the voluntary units of Shkodër and the Malcijas. He had sent me sincere greetings and word that he had heard of these false accusations, and that I should not worry as he knew our patriotic feelings and that these enemies could not harm us. For the moment, they had stopped the enemy and would continue to do so until we won. I told the bajraktar that Kel had got his passport and left, but that I was worried about myself. Even if they arrested me, they weren't going to finish me, but I didn't want to give our enemies the satisfaction, as we were greater Albanians at heart than they were. We worked and fought for it, putting our interests and position in jeopardy when Albania was under Ottoman Empire rule.

Gjon stayed for lunch with us. As he left, I asked him to give my warmest regards to Sulco Bey, and to tell him that if things were in his hands or people like him, it would be better for us and to not worry. However, nowadays, things are in the hands of those who act not knowing our hearts and political views, and I will have to act on things as they come up as I see fit.

Rumours spread in Shkodër that the volunteers of the Committee of Podgorica plundered and burned wherever they went. The population of Shkodër revolted, and wanted to pull down the houses of all Slavophiles. They started with Luk Lukaj's house, and pulled down the roof tiles. It wasn't his house though, he was only renting. Then they did the same to Alush Lohja's house. They planned to come to ours too, but Kolë was out at the time and heard of it in advance. We immediately placed our armed guards in front of our house so that nobody could approach. Armed manservants were also placed outside the walls.

We sent word to Monsignor Serreqi, Shuk and Dr. Rauf Angoni that we were not going to let anyone come near the house, and that we would defend ourselves. We also sent urgent word to the Malcija of Shkreli. We asked that the authorities in Shkodër stop the insurgents that had incited the people of Shkodër to violence. The police took severe measures dispersing the demonstrators, and sent them home. For three days, our guards and manservants held their posts, day and night. You, my dear children, for sure do not remember this event, except perhaps Zina, who was the oldest.

On the third day, I went with Palokë, Pjetër Marashi, our cousin's son (Gasper), and the armed escort to see another cousin's son, Sokrat [Socrat], at his hotel, the Hotel Grand, where we stayed for a while. There, I heard that the authorities had wanted to arrest the Llulojts, but the residents of Dudosis (part of Shkodër) had all gathered to prevent it. They all belonged to Essad Pasha Toptani's political party. This spoiled my visit as I got worried and anxious. The political situation was very uncertain.

77

On our way back, we ran into Bajram Bey Curri, his grandson Husein, and his armed escort. We had not seen each other since 1919 in Vienna. We greeted each other warmly, but nevertheless, he reproached me for not visiting him sooner as he had been in Shkodër for two weeks. Per the customs of the time, it was obligatory for me to return this visit. I explained that lately we'd had many worries and problems, but that he was right. He replied that he knew, but still had looked forward to it, as he wanted to talk with me about something he'd heard. I promised I would visit in the afternoon.

It was past noon when we got home, and everybody was worried about us. I got a telegram from Kel letting us know that he'd had a good trip and was well in Dubrovnik. In the afternoon, Palokë, Mirash Luca, our armed escort, and I went to pay a visit to Bajram Bey. Kolë stayed home to take care of the house and family.

When we arrived, we found quite a crowd including people from Kosovo, Malcorë, and Shkodrians, most of which were Roman Catholic. They took us to the room where Bajram Bey was. After the hearty greetings and courteous inquiries about family life, and how he was feeling, he said that he was feeling like any refugee who had to leave his land.

Bajram Bey Curri, 1920s [PD]

We spoke about kismet, and the days we had spent in Vienna together, and the good times we had there. He told me that Dr. Farija had told him of our troubles of late. Dr. Farija was a well known physician from Kosovo and friend of ours who had suffered for his politics and patriotism before the liberation of Albania, and later from Zog's regime. I let Bajram Bey know that they had accused us of being dangerous as Slavophiles, and that I was worried. Bajram Bey got mad at Ahmet and told me:

> "Mr, Shkreli, do not feel distressed. The real patriots know you very well, and how you have always been devoted to the welfare of our country, supported its interests, often putting yours in jeopardy, because of your social and political influence. All your efforts towards the betterment of our people were voluntary. Why should Amhet's regime accuse us of being Slavophiles, which is normal in order to be good neighbours and Balkanians, when he himself, since 1915, was connected with the Serbs in Nis, and as late as 1919 in Vienna had belonged to Essad Pasha Toptani's Party, the same as us. Mr.

Shkreli, thank you very much for your visit. My house is always open to you and your family whatever the occasion, especially if it suddenly becomes necessary to meet in an emergency. If you like and feel safer, come and stay with me. There is no person alive that I would allow to harm you and yours as long as I am alive".

I replied:

"I am pleased, Bajram Bey, for your sympathy, strong feelings and noble generosity, and for that I thank you from the bottom of my heart. I do not want to cause trouble for anybody, or to stay under their protection. I've received the same offer from some members of the political party Popullore, but I have made up my mind to not give the satisfaction to our enemies. As soon as I see that there is danger for me to be interned, I know what I am going to do. I am Malcorë, Bajram Bey, like you. We will never surrender when we know we are innocent".

We embraced each other, promising to meet again. On our way back home, we walked a bit around the center of Shkodër. The next day was the day of the pazar [bazaar, outdoor market] when you had to buy all the provisions for the week. As Kolë took care of that, I told him not to go with our carriage, as usual, but with a manservant in a public carriage, so as not to be noticed. Even Pina, Nine and the children seldom went out in our carriages now, for the same reason.

When we returned home, we found visitors had come to see us: Shuk (my wife's uncle), Zef Shiroka and Ndrek Kiçi. They confirmed that the word had circulated around Shkodër about the arrests, but did not believe them as they were sure Shkodër would not allow Tiranë to have its way. After the guests had gone, the family gathered and decided that I should stay hidden with Shuk's family for a few days. I chose Shuk's house as it was the largest, and could hide me better as it was surrounded with neighbours who were friends. So if I had to flee, I could easily go from garden to garden to leave Shkodër. If the authorities came to my house for me, the family would say that they do not know where I am, and that I had discovered the authorities intentions and left Shkodër. I promised my family that before I left, we would meet again.

Shuk Serreqi's house [M2]

Chapter 7: Leaving Albania

As I left our house, I was distressed and had the unpleasant feeling that this might be forever. The prophecy was correct. I felt sad and my heart ached for Nine and children. Joseph was only five months old. I'd hardly had any time to enjoy with him. That was the fate of politicians who tried all their life to help their fellow beings, and were always true to their ideals. This way was better for the family too. Palokë and our cousin's son (Gasper) accompanied me to Shuk's place without bodyguards, in order to be less conspicuous. Shuk had already been informed and was waiting for me. I told him that I had decided to leave Shkodër. Shuk thought that I should still wait to see what Tiranë was going to do. First we should speak with Monsignor Serreqi, then I could decide.

Baba Gasper, came the next morning, as we'd sent word where I was. After visiting, he went to see Nine and the children. About noon, Palokë came to tell me that one of our three business partners in Shkodër had refused to return the capital we had invested with him. In our vineyards, we had invested in partners to make the wine and raki [brandy]. Word had spread that I had left Shkodër, and soon the other two partners joined in. They took advantage of our political situation and refused to return our investment, which was a considerable sum of money. All three had been Kel's friends.

I have always been against partnerships, but Kel insisted and I gave in. This unexpected event was very upsetting, but did not finish us off financially. Although during the Austro-Hungarian occupation, our family started to lose money, as they had taken so much and given in return some bonds worth less than a third of the value. Because of the continued fighting between the volunteers of Shkodër and the Committee of Podgorica, we had also given the volunteers of Shkodër our wooden barrels to carry water and whatever else they needed at the front line. But still, we could endure these losses.

In the evening, Kolë came and I gave him instructions about the administration and management of our estate and properties as well as the care of the family and other advice in case I had to leave Albania. If it happened, he was to go immediately to Monsignor Serreqi, as according to Albanian law, no action could be taken against them, when only women and children remained in a house. I gave him all the keys, instructed him to keep one carriage in Shkodër for the ladies and children, and not to use the others.

After Kolë left, Shuk came and told me that Malo Bey Bushati, the chief of police, and Ymer Lutfia [Lutfi], the chief of the gendarmerie, had sent word to me that they did not have any orders from Ahmet against me. If they got any, they would notify me, while they pretend they are looking for me. As it was Sunday, I went with Shuk, Baba Gasper and Palokë to attend mass at the Roman Catholic cathedral. It seems word had already spread that I was in hiding, as the people in church stared at me in surprise. As we left, many people came to shake our hands. Then we went to the archdiocese, which was in the same complex, to see Monsignor Serreqi.

Clockwise from top left: unknown, Zef Serreqi, Ali Hoxha, Luigj Gërxhola, Zef
Mirditë, Malo Bey Bushati, unknown, Ibrahim Mandiqi & Ymer Lutfia [M1]

Monsignor Serreqi said to me:

> "Nush, I see that you have made up your mind to leave Shkodër and go to
> Dubrovnik, and then for sure to Belgrade where you will meet members of the
> Yugoslav government and the Prime Minister Pašić. Tell them that they can't
> engage in politics with Alush Lohja and Luk Lukaj. They should have chosen
> better people. Shkodër would not agree to any understandings as long as
> Yugoslavia is represented by them. Shkodër is not a rug to be thrown around.
> Shkodër has its proud and magnificent history, and is the most powerful city
> in Albania."

I answered:

> "Both sides have made mistakes. Shkodër is divided into many political
> factions and opinions instead of having one leader, that has the ability to lead,
> to look after its interests, as well as those of North Albania. It is split into
> hundreds of leaders. The Committee of Podgorica has taken advantage of this
> split and, at the same time, has jeopardized Yugoslav political friendship with
> Albania, and pushed Shkodër into the grasp of Tiranë and South Albania.
> Never will Shkodër be able to overcome this setback. It will become a slave,
> subject to the will of Tiranë.

81

Uncle Jak, I will go to Belgrade as I have to settle some obstacles regarding a partnership we have in Dubrovnik, and while there, will talk with the Yugoslav authorities about the error done in their supporting the Committee of Podgorica. We had the agreement with Yugoslavia that they would be friends of Albania. But because of this, all we who are Slavophiles are persecuted by our authorities. We bear unjust consequences, endangering our wealth and positions, for our valiant generosity and the help offered to the Serbian army in their difficult time, retreating through Albania in 1916. The Yugoslav Minister in Shkodër, Ljuba Nešić, as well as the Yugoslav supreme army headquarters and most of the Ministers were also against this Committee of Podgorica."

He said:

"My dear Nush, I pity Nine, Pina and your children who have to suffer because of your political views. As for you and Kel, since you have embraced this cause and will carry on, you are deceiving yourselves as your are too honest and gullible. In this way, you are going to sacrifice all you own."

He was a real prophet. I answered:

"You see, Uncle Jak, I am Shkodranian, an Albanian and a Malcorë, and it is with great sorrow that I leave, but I am forced against my will. For Kel and I, leaving Albania is the end of our political lives. We have conducted gallant, brave and bold politics, as have done our ancestors, on our own expenses, and not as it is done nowadays to get paid for it. You know how ruined Kel's health is. His years are numbered. But Shkodër's Malcija leadership whose independent governing up until now was recognized by all past governments, has come to an end. From now on, they will be under Tiranë's rule."

Monsignor Serreqi embraced me, wished me prosperity and success and gave me his pastoral blessings. This was the last time we saw each other. He died in 1922, disappointed as Shkodër fell to the fate I predicted.

When we parted, Baba Gasper, Shuk, Palokë and I went to our house for dinner. Our cousin's son (Gasper) arrived with a message from Malo Bey and Ymer Lutfia, saying that I should take care of myself and not be seen around as they both had to go to Koplik for a couple of days, and were afraid that during their absence some order might arrive from Ahmet's government. Hearing that, Shuk said that, by all means, I should go with him to his house, and from there leave Shkodër if it became necessary. The family council decided for me that it would be best if I did leave Shkodër, as the situation was critical. When it was dark, I took leave of Nine and our children, as well as Pina and my nephew and neice. You, my children, when you read this will yourselves be parents and comprehend how heartbroken I was, and what degree of pain I felt taking leave from you and your mother.

Serreqi Family: (left-right, top down) Lecë, Luigj, Ejell, Baba Gasper, Filip, Shuk, Gjon, Adusha, Zef; Age, Rosë, Monsignor Jak, Drande, Gasper Jr., Zina; Maria, Cinë. [FAM]

Ymer Lutfia [M1]

Kolë, Palokë and our cousin's son (Gasper) accompanied me to Shuk's. I arranged with Palokë to come the next day with two of our horses, and my hunting suit, as if we were going to hunt. Shuk tried hard to make me change my mind, but I

had decided to leave Shkodër and Albania in order to not cause any trouble for Shuk's family, as well as to not be caught in a trap.

At daybreak on Monday the 21st of August, dressing in hunting suits, Palokë and I mounted the horses and left Shuk's house and Shkodër. The night before, we had sent two of our bodyguards to let the Peci's in the village of Kaç [Kaçë / Kaca / Kaci, in the Zadrimë province of Albania] know we were coming, as they were our first stop. Palokë and I took the route along the Kiri River to where Kolë was waiting for us. Again, I entrusted the care of the family and estate to Kolë.

As we left, we turned back towards Shkodër to have one last look. Deep in my heart, I had a feeling of immense sorrow and fear, that maybe I was leaving the place of my birth, youth and adulthood for a very long time, maybe even forever, and I wanted to keep a picture of it in my mind. We continued along the Drin [Drini / Drina / Drinasa] River, then left it and entered Zadrimë province, where I spent a couple of days. When we entered, Dodë [Dod] Peci met us in person with his sons, and welcomed us with the characteristic words used on these occasions, "Welcome and thank you Mr. Nush to have honoured us by choosing our house. Come in please, you are now under our besa".

We had visited each other many times before World War I, as we were friends and had to go through Zadrimë when the family went to visit the family of Pjeter Mirashi in Grumin, or to Ana e Malit, where we had our livestock. Zadrimë is one of the most beautiful of Shkodër county's provinces, with fertile fields, as well as numerous vineyards and orchards. When we arrived at Dodë Peci's house in Kaç, we were greeted by his brothers and others. As soon as their cousins heard of our arrival, they came to greet us too. After that, the ladies of the house and the children left us alone. Dinner was served and we started talking.

I told them about the situation in Shkodër and Koplik, and how many people from Koplik and the surrounding areas had to escape to Shkodër. Dodë responded by saying that they too had heard this, and Monsignor Koleci, the Roman Catholic Archbishop of Zadrimë, had called them all to persuade them to support the government's side. But, they had refused, as they hadn't any agreement with Tiranë, which at the time had governing power over Shkodër. Monsignor Koleci had not liked it, because the clergy had already made an agreement with the authorities in Tiranë. The people of Zadrimë had also suffered injustices and abuses many times and nobody helped them defend their rights.

Before we retired for the night, we decided that Palokë and Kolë should return to Shkodër the next day, accompanied by a cousin of the Peci family. I suggested to them that if anybody asked them where they had been, they could say that Palokë had gone to Zadrimë to look at his lands and vineyards and Kolë had gone to Ana e Malit to inspect the livestock we have there. The Peci family sent a message with them to the Shkreli ladies, "Do not worry about Mr. Nush, he is in the house of Pecis and the Peci family is not afraid of the Matianian" (Ahmet Zog was from Mati in North Albania).

Early the next morning, I went with Palokë and Kolë to pay a visit to Dodë's cousins and uncle. We stayed for lunch at Ndrek Peci's house, who received us with all honours and esteem, as required by an honorable family such as theirs. After the meal, Palokë and Kolë got ready to leave for Shkodër. I embraced them and was in low spirits as I had a foreboding that years would pass before I saw my homeland again. I asked them again to take care of the family and to remind my cousin's son (Gasper) to go to Nešić (the Yugoslav Minister), to get me permission to enter Yugoslavia. We arranged for Gasper to meet up with me in Zadrimë the next Thursday.

On Tuesday afternoon, I walked around the village with Dodë. When we returned to his house, we found Dodë's cousins. They informed him of the rumour that the authorities of Tiranë were sending a unit to subjugate Zadrimë. The people of Zadrimë had given their besa to resist.

On Wednesday, which was the day of the pazar in Shkodër, I went out in the street to watch the picturesque crowd of men and women in their national clothes and the horses and donkeys loaded with agricultural products to be taken to Shkodër. The same trade route was used by traders from Mirditë on their way to Shkodër.

On Thursday 26 August 1920, Palokë came to me in Kaç, bringing news from the family that they were all well, but that rumour had spread in Shkodër about my departure as no one had seen me lately. The authorities got suspicious too, and instructed the police stations to find out where I was. Because of that, I went with Palokë to Bushat, to stay a few days with our cousin Ndocë's son, Zef Shkreli. Don Zef was the Roman Catholic parson at the Bushat's Parish. He was delighted to see me (the feeling was mutual), and even more so as his sister (Ganxhe) and her son were also visiting. We were all very glad to see each other, especially me, knowing that I would not see them again for a very long time, if ever.

Don Zef Shkreli [M2]

When we came back to the Peci's house in Kaç, Palokë departed for Shkodër with my advice for the family. I remained in Kaç, and walked around the village with Dodë. My mind was filled with thoughts of my family, and of ways to cross the border. When we returned, I found a letter from Nine, letting me know that everybody at home was well and that I should not worry about them, but instead I should take care of myself and to try not to be seen much. She also wrote that the authorities had deduced that I had left. They had not yet procured the permit for me to enter Yugoslavia, as nobody dared to approach the Yugoslav

Consulate because of the political situation. The Yugoslav Consul himself spent most of his time in Shiroka [Shirokë, a village near Shkodër]. The consul had sent word that if I could come to Shiroka, the permission to enter Dubrovnik was waiting for me there.

I was very happy to see Nine's handwriting, and hearing that everybody was well, as I was very worried that the authorities in Shkodër and Tiranë would disturb them. The letter was brought by one of our bodyguards (they had all remained in Shkodër to protect our family and house).

On Sunday morning, I went with Dodë, his brother and sons to Mergj for the feast of Saint Kryëpremit, their patron saint. It was a magnificent festival, as well as a meeting for the social and political leaders of the province. The government of Tiranë had not yet subjugated Zadrimë, and the people there did not acknowledge its authority. They first wanted to see how the political situation developed. At the time, they still recognized the government of Durrës (due to the liberation of Albania from the Ottoman Empire in Durrës in 1912).

The chaplain in Mergj held mass in the church, but started to involve politics in his sermon, as the clergy had already recognized the authorities in Tiranë. The Zadrinians silenced him immediately and started to leave the church. The priest understood that he had gone to far, and to lessen his error, finished the mass in a hurry. We met this priest again at lunch in the leading house of Mergj, where we had both been invited. This priest had the audacity to approach me, excusing himself that he had not recognized me as he had not seen me for so many years, and saying that otherwise he would not have involved politics in his sermon. He was just afraid that I would relay his words to Dodë and at the same time, he was afraid of his superiors.

During the meal, the converstation turned negatively toward the religious leaders who had gotten involved in politics, and how they were causing dissentions among the people. I interrupted, and being their guest and in their besa, they listened to me. I calmed them down with a patriotic historical speech. The first to leave was the priest, who as it later came out, had gone directly to the Roman Catholic Bishop of Zadrimë, Monsignor Koleci [Kolecë], whose diocese was in Nënshat.

On Monday morning, a troop of horsemen could be seen approaching Kaç. The men of Kaç got alarmed, mounted their horses and rode out to meet the cavalcade, thinking that the government had sent its gendarmerie to subjugate them. Dodë said to me, "Don't worry Nush. At the first shot, the whole village will attack them. No matter how strong they are, none of them will enter Kaç alive". Thank God that there was no need for bloodshed. The cavalcade turned out to be Monsignor Koleci, escorted by his manservants, and two men from his village.

As they approached, we drew nearer to greet them. Seeing me, the Monsignor pretended to be surprised that I was in Zadrimë, and asked, "How are you getting on with Dodë? Did you soften him up or aggravate him further?". I answered, "No need for either Monsignor, as he who behaves himself near Dodë has no need to fear him". The Monsignor interrupted me saying, "But Dodë is like a wolf with me and never listened to my words". Later in the house of Dodë, as the Monsignor was his guest too, we confirmed that the priest that left the meal had indeed gone to tell him that I was staying with Dodë, and about the speech I had made at the banquet. It seemed this speech had pleased the Monsignor but he still wanted to personally verify that I had not come to pit Zadrimë against the government of Tiranë.

Maybe you, my children, will be surprised at the fact that everybody in the villages and Roman Catholic clergy had known that I was at Dodë Peci's house, yet nobody informed the authorities. You see, they would not and could not, as everyone there knew what I was in the besa of the Peci family, and they would never break their besa. It would have only lead to bloodshed.

We all had long conversations with Monsignor Koleci, as he was Dodë's guest the whole day, before returning home. When the Monsignor and I were left alone for a while, he told me that he had a message for me from Monsignor Serreqi:

> "Monsignor Serreqi sent word for you that in the interests of your family, and because you made up your mind to leave Albania, it would be best for them that you leave as soon as possible. Word has spread that you came to Zadrimë for the sole purpose of raising a rebellion against the government of Tiranë. You know as well as we do that this was not your intention, so why keep alive those false accusations against you by staying in Zadrimë, and maybe giving someone else a chance for political ploys".

I agreed with all he said. I had to leave immediately. We took a hearty leave from each other, hoping to meet again. We met once more, eight years later in Vienna. Later on, he too was disappointed in Ahmet Zog's politics. Before Monsignor Koleci took leave from Dodë, he informed him that for the next day, he had summoned all the elders of Zadrimë in a conference. He was going to try to change their minds, to recognize the government of Tiranë. Zadrimë, being a wealthy and powerful province of North Albania, did not feel threatened by not recognizing the government of Tiranë.

When Dodë returned the next day from the conference, he informed me in detail of the discussions that had taken place. He said the elders of had declared that they would be honoured if I would consent to stay permanently in Zadrimë, and be their delegate and represent them on official occasions. Dodë had answered to this proposal, "Even though a loyal patriot, Nush Shkreli would not accept it. He has decided to go and live in other parts of Europe, as he has had enough of life in Shkodër because of political enemies and the injustices that dominate there". After this message, he advised me to leave for Dubrovnik, as I had business there and had already made up my mind to go. He told me that if Kel and I decided to come back to Albania, I had his word that we could be their delegates.

I thanked him for his trust and the honour they showed us. I also expressed my doubts about our return in the near future because of the bad political situation, the discord and division among the provinces, the Malcijas and the clergy, all one against another. Our family bore the greatest damage and losses due to envy and jealousy of some Catholics in Shkodër who accused us of liking the Serbs more than our own countrymen. They were totally wrong. For us, Albania and its welfare always came first. We also supported friendly relations with the neighbouring countries, although we did not want to be under their control.

There were many visitors that day at Dodë's house, and we spent the time discussing politics. Dodë invited some guests for dinner and an overnight stay. I had the special satisfaction of being able to talk openly with all these elders. That was my last night in Zadrimë and my last meeting and discussion with their leaders. I had chosen their independent province to avoid being discovered by the cunning spies of Ahmet Zog's government. I will always remember the provinces of Zadrimë and Kaya, where the Peci family have their residences, and the Peci's sincere, cordial friendship and their besa and courage.

The 1st of September in 1920 was my last night at the Peci's house. That night we retired very late, passing the time in conversation. About noon on the next day, Palokë came from Shkodër and brought me a letter from Nine. She informed me that everybody was well and that I should not worry. She wrote that the children had sent me their love, thinking I had gone on a trip like at other times. Thank God that the innocent little ones continued their daily lives undisturbed. She wrote that every day her father, Baba Gasper, Uncles Shuk & Filip, Shan Koleka and Bep Muxhani came to see them. Palokë usually spent the nights in our house to support the family. Dr. Rauf Bey Angoni also came often, as well as other relatives and friends.

After informing me about our house and property, she also let me know that the Gendarmerie of Shkodër had sent its gendarmes to look for me. They gave her a written order to be handed to me that I had 24 hours to report to the authorities in Shkodër, otherwise they were going to take steps against me. At first, Nine and Pina were scared, but Shuk sent her word that the authorities would not take action against the other family members. Nine advised me to leave Zadrimë as soon as possible.

The authorities in Shkodër were of the opinion that I was organizing a resistance toward the government of Tiranë and their authorities in Shkodër. The commandant of the gendarmerie in Shkodër was Malo Bey Bushati. After he got the order from Ahmet in Tiranë, being a friend of our family, he did the honourable thing. Instead of sending the gendarmes to surround our house and search it, as was the custom of the time, he sent his secretary Mr. Luigi Garzhola, to hand my wife the order. Mr. Garzhola whispered to my wife to inform me that Malo Bey's advice was that I should leave Albania immediately, but to be careful as the authorities were blocking the exits. He also wished me good luck.

My wife advised me that I should leave Kaç and cross the border. She reproached me for being seen walking around the village, as this behaviour had alarmed the authorities in Tiranë. Kel also wanted to know where I was. She assured me that I should not worry about the family as they were protected by their kin and many friends of the family. Palokë also passed on some money she sent me. Dodë assured me that nothing could happen to me while I was still in Zadrimë, as they were all behind me. I thanked him, and we started to plan which route I should take and settled on going along the bank of the Buna [Bojana] River. We had our lunch. Palokë rode back to Shkodër, and I went with Dodë and Ndrek Peci and two of their kin from Kaç toward Kosmače (Montenegro), and entered the village of Bërdicë [Brdica].

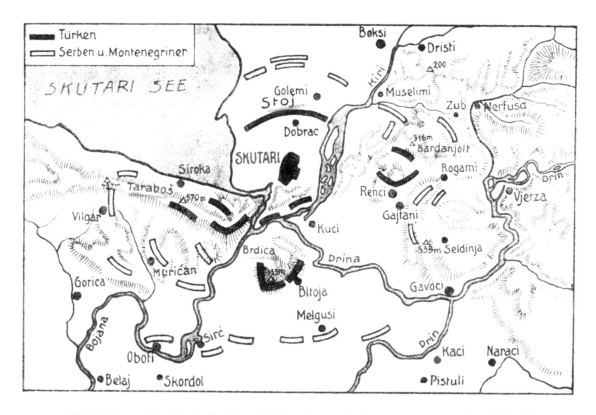

1913 Map of Turkish, Serbian & Montenegrin forces surrounding Shkodër, showing villages & rivers in the area [From Albanian Shkodër Balkankrieg]

In Bërdicë we had good friends, the powerful family of Alihebe. Bërdicë is only a one hour horse ride from Shkodër, and the proximity made me nostalgic and long to see my family. I remembered the quote, "What did I do to you Shkodër that you are sending me again away to wander about foreign lands. Am I not your son too?", though I didn't recall the author. Only, in my case, it was not Shkodër's fault that I had to leave, but of some impudent people who could not stand our promoting the rights of women, modernizing our way of life and doing away with old prejudices, as well being envious of our powerful social, economic and political positions.

I had taken this route through Bërdicë many times on my way to Istanbul, Ismir and Thessaloniki, or going to weddings in Bërdicë, Bushat, Barbullush, Kolaj, Shëngjin and Lezhë. After we left Alihebe's house and Bërdicë, we continued on to the Palokaj family's house. They received us cordially, as they were friends of Dodë Peci. After hearing about my situation and finding out that I was Gasper's brother, they became even more friendly as they had been his friend too. They wanted us to stay at least a

89

couple of days with them, but we declined their invitation. Thanking them warmly, Dodë explained that we had to continue our travels before dawn.

Our mother's cousin, Don Zef Gurakuqi, had in the distant past been the parson, a Catholic priest of Beltojë [Beltoj / Bltoja]. He was esteemed and still remembered by the folks there. The head of the house of Palokaj called his mother to meet me, as I was the nephew of Don Zef. We stayed for a short visit, then the master of the house escorted us with his men to Shirq [Shirgj / Sirć]. There, we went to the house of Mark Kini, friends of the Dodë's, and of the Çeka's, so we were warmly welcomed. Here I had to part from Dodë Peci and the others that had accompanied us. With immense feelings of sadness, Dodë and I took leave from each other, as if we foresaw we would never meet again.

In Zadrimë, the family of Peci is one of the most powerful and important in the province and have played a political role as if they were Malcorë. They later came into conflict with Ahmet's government, which wanted to subjugate Zadrimë, and Dodë Peci would not allow it. One day, returning from Lezhë, he was attacked and wounded by the authorities. He resisted as long as he had ammunition, and with the last cartridge, killed himself. I was already in Dubrovnik when I heard this, and it made me very sad.

In Shirq, Mark Kini invited me to stay with his family as long as I wished, declaring that there was no power that could capture me while in his besa. I thanked him with all my heart, but declined the offer. I did not want to cause them trouble. Also, I was planning to cross the border shortly, so I only spent that day and night in Mark Kini's house. The next day, in the afternoon, Mark and some members of his family accompanied me as we crossed the river Buna. There, I took my leave as they had to return home, and I had a journey to continue.

Chapter 8: Dubrovnik

Until the Paris Peace Conference of 1920, Albania did not have today's borders, so Ana e Malit and Tarabosh [Taraboš], near Shkodër, were under Yugoslav occupation. Once there, I asked the military authorities to give me an escort to Shirokë, on Shkodër Lake. I felt safe there, and not in a hurry anymore as I was out of reach of Ahmet's regime.

From Ana e Malit, I could see Shkodër. My thoughts were of my wife and children. I wondered how long it would take the courier sent by Mark Kini to inform them and Kolë that I made it to Shirokë. I had many friends there. Among them was a faithful lady who I asked to go to Shkodër to see my wife and deliver a message that I was in Shirokë. On her way back from Shkodër a couple of days later, she brought me some clothes, money and the information that the majority of the members of Essad Pasha's political party had been arrested.

That afternoon I returned to the hotel after some visits with friends. Mr. Sterkić, from the Yugoslav consulate in Shkodër, was waiting for me. I asked why they did not send the permit for me to enter Yugoslavia when I was in Zadrimë. He answered that they could not as nobody dared approach the Yugoslav Consulate in Shkodër, and he didn't think the border guards would stop my passage here. The next day, the secretary of the Yugoslav Consulate in Shkodër, Mr. Ivo Vukotić, came and brought me the permit. I had lunch with him and Mr. Sterkić. Ivo had started his diplomatic career with Ljuba Nešić.

My wife had informed me that Malo Bey Bushati had proved to be a sincere and faithful friend, so before I left Shirokë, I wrote a letter to him saying, among other things:

> "I am not escaping from my country but only distancing myself from it. Only thieves, murderers and criminals escape. The politicians and honest people distance themselves. They don't surrender to enemies and dictators that rely on accusations and denunciations of their enemies, and unscrupulous and irresponsible employees. In order to not satisfy someone else's wishes to humiliate and harass me, dragging me through the courts and prisons, I am leaving the country that I love more than the ones who now govern it and call themsleves patriots and nationalists.
>
> Malo Bey, please inform the Minister and government that Nush Shkreli was once deceived, stayed and was interned by the Austro-Hungarian authorities when they occupied Albania during World War I. I am not going to let that happen a second time. The authorities should have properly and thoroughly checked the accusations against us, and then they would have realized that they could not be true. This is not the way to run a country if you wish to succeed and achieve a proper and just government. Today, I crossed the border and entered Yugoslavia, where I intend to stay until justice reigns in my country."

With that letter, I wanted to justify my actions in order to not seem to be involved in dealings I had no part in. I didn't want to be considered a refugee avoiding a court of justice, but seeing the injustice, chose to distance myself from it. With the word "distance", I also wanted to protect my family, as this word did not have the consequences that the word "refugee" would. Later, when we met again, Malo Bey told me that he had informed Ahmet as soon as he got the letter. Ahmet replied, "Why didn't Nush come to see me before he left the country?".

After I boarded the ship in Shirokë, and was buying the ticket to Rijeka Crnojevića, Don Pjeter saw me and advised me to buy a ticket that went to Plavnic, as it was a shorter route to Cetinje. When I disembarked in Plavnic, I realized he'd tricked me, as waiting there for me were Alush Lohja and Luk Lukaj. Our family had already broken up with Alush as we didn't approve of his line of politics, and I'd only met Luk once, when he came to Shkodër with his lies about working as Essad Pasha's assistant.

Alush approached me to welcome and congratulate me for having escaped from Ahmet. I replied that I was only on my way to Dubrovnik. Alush insisted that we visit at his house, which was nearby, to have a cup of coffee, or else he would be offended. I had no choice but to accept. When they started talking about the war though, I interrupted, saying, "We have nothing to say about that with you, as Kel and I and all the others that wish the best for Albania and friendly relations with Yugoslavia are against the attacks by the Committee of Podgorica. Kel and I will never forgive you for the matter between us, in which you sent falsified telegrams in our name". They pretended that the Committee of Podgorica had sent these telegrams without consulting with them. As soon as I finished the coffee, I left. I was very angry with Don Pjeter, the hypocrite, because this visit was against our interests and he was supposed to be Kel's friend. He came to visit us again, but I never spoke to him again.

From Podgorica, I continued to Dubrovnik through Cetinje and Kotor. In Cetinje, I met General Draza Mihajlović, the supreme commander of the Yugoslav army in Crna Gora [Montenegro]. We discussed the political errors that were happening frequently. Instead of strengthening relations between the Albanian people and its government, it just led to misunderstandings and hostile relations with the Slav people. He was of the same opinion and criticized his Ministry of External Affairs. He expressed his regrets for the unpleasantness our family was facing, and congratulated me for having crossed the border safely. He also asked if I had been well received by the Yugoslav military at the border.

General Draza Mihajlović, 1943 [PD]

92

I thanked him for the warm and courteous welcome I received from the Yugoslav military. He then informed me that he had sent the War Minister in Belgrade a detailed report of all the errors made by the Committee of Podgorica, as it affected the honour of the military forces of Yugoslavia. Then we parted ways. The next day, I continued towards Kotor.

When I arrived, the ship from Dubrovnik had just docked. Minister Ljuba Nešić, was on that ship. He was on his way from Belgrade to Albania. In Dubrovnik, he had met my brother, Kel. He told me that Kel was worried about me. Ljuba and I had dinner together, and engaged in a long talk. The next day, I left for Dubrovnik to meet up with Kel. It was a great joy for me when I was reunited with him.

In Dubrovnik, I found many serious issues with our business partner there. He had committed many errors, and caused us huge losses. We also had many acquaintances from Shkodër there, who were political exiles that had borrowed money from Kel, about a thousand gold Napoleons. But, it was clear to me that we'd never get that money back either, and we never did.

Kel and I went to Belgrade on business and stayed there about two months. Kel's health deteriorated, so we returned to Dubrovnik. Meanwhile, Christmas had arrived, and besides the time we were interned during World War I, this was the first time we didn't celebrate at home. We celebrated instead in the Imperial Hotel, where we were staying. In the afternoon on Christmas Day, we paid a visit to the Mati Vierdha family. After New Year's Day, Kel's health got worse. When he'd recovered a bit, I went with him to Vienna, to consult Dr. Ortner, a professor and renowned specialist of internal medecine. He advised Kel to go to Semmering, a health resort near Vienna, for three months. I took Kel there, and after a couple of days, as Kel got better, I left for Dubrovnik by way of Vienna, then Belgrade. After three months, Kel was recovered enough and returned to Dubrovnik too.

It was clear that we would not be returning to Albania in the near future, so we decided to bring our wives and children to Dubrovnik and wrote them a letter regarding that. Baba Gasper, Uncle Shuk and Palokë helped them sell the house. Pina and Nine left some of the most valuable things with their families, and other things they sold or donated. Our lands, livestock and other possessions we entrusted to the people who already managed them. The big trunks [luggage] were sent to Dubrovnik by ship. So, in the summer of 1921, our families left Shkodër for good.

Our wives and children, along with Kolë and his sister, Gjyste, came in our carriages through Ulqin, Tivar, and Kotor on their way to Dubrovnik. Kel and I had already rented a big house, and bought the furniture. We kept one of the carriages with two horses for ourselves. Although the upkeep was pretty expensive, I did not want to disappoint Kel, as he was in poor health and could not walk easily. I also didn't want him to realize that were were continuously having financial losses. I had no heart to worry him about this, knowing that he didn't have long left to live. When Kolë came, he informed me that the business partnerships we had in Shkodër had lost all the money we had there. We also liquidated what was left in our warehouses, and lost a lot of money there too. As Albania didn't yet have status as an independent country, we could not claim war damages using the receipts the Austro-Hungarian army gave us for what they took.

Clockwise from top-left: Pina, Joseph, Nine, Gita, Zana, Ndoci, Zela and Zina, 1921
[FAM]

In January 1920, Kel went to Belgrade and got in touch with the Yugoslav Prime Minister, Nikola Pašić. He spoke to him about the war receipts, and it was decided Kel should make a petition to the Yugoslav Ministry of Foreign Affairs for help, as we had been in the committe that had helped the Serbian army during their retreat through Albania. Kel was to include the original receipts, and to request collection of the war damages. Kel did so and handed it in to the Ministry office dealing with these things, and was given a receipt for the submitted documents. Months, and then years passed by and we didn't get anything from the Ministry. We regularly inquired to find out the result, but all in vain. At last after many years, the petition was found but the war receipts were missing. We never found out who cashed those war receipts, which were worth 3,000 gold Napoleons. Poor Kel, till the last moment of his life, he kept inquiring about the money. I always tried to lessen his worry.

That was another case of our bad luck, and someone stealing our money. At least we had the great joy of being reunited with our family. The children, thank God, were all well. Joseph was already a year old. I took Zina, Gita and Ndoci to Vienna to continue their schooling. Zina and Gita went to the College of Saint Crucifix in Rodaun and Ndoci went to the college of the Jesuits in Kalksburg, both near Vienna. Zana, Zela and Joseph were still small and remainded at home, to our great pleasure. Zela, being the most courageous, was the commander of the other two.

In the spring of 1922, Kel went to Vienna with Pina to visit Zina, Gita and Ndoci in their colleges, and to see Kel's doctors. On the doctors' advice, they spent two months in Semmering (near vienna) at a health resort. Whatever money could buy, I provided for my poor brother to prolong his life. To our great sorrow though, in the autumn of 1924, he died. I lost my last brother. His death was a deep blow to us, but life had to go on.

In Dubrovnik, Nine and I had another son and we called him Mati. He was a healthy and happy boy. Joseph was fond of him, as were Zana, Zela and the rest of us. To our deep sorrow, when he was a year and a half old, he got meningitis, and died. After a couple of years, I transported Kel and Mati's bodies to our family tomb in Shkodër.

After Kel's death, Pina's brother (Palokë), and their sister came from Shkodër to Dubrovnik. Palokë extended his stay with us to help determine what property remained. When Kel died, our properties in Shkodër were already diminished. As always happens when the owers are away, everything goes wrong. The fields don't yield properly, the livestock got several diseases, etc. Everything was deteriorating. The business in Dubrovnik did not go well either. Dubrovnik was not a good place for business, but I could not leave initially because of Kel's illness, and later on, it was too late. What we had left was divided in two parts: half for Pina, Ndoci and Zana, and half for me and my family.

Pina was to return with her children and brother to Albania but she refused. She wanted to stay with me and my family. Although it would have been easier with only one family to worry about, I took the responsibility for Kel's too, for the love I had for him. As there was no longer any hope of returning to Albania, I put all the children in Yugoslav schools to learn the language, and get ready for life. We stayed in Dubrovnik until the autumn of 1929.

When our father traveled through Kosovo, he often had the opportunity to go to Gjakova and became friends with the Kryeziu family [The Bey's of Kosovo]. Riza Bey Kryeziu had been a great patriot and fought for the liberation of Albania from Ottoman domination. He was fearless and bold at a meeting in the Saraj in Istanbul, where he got up and exclaimed, "Long live free Albania!". This utterance had bad consequences for his family though. His sons were: Ali Bey, Ceno Bey, Hasan Bey, Gani Bey, and Said Bey. In politics, the first one to succeed him was Ceno [Cena] Bey, and after his assassination, Gani Bey.

Gani Bey Kryeziu, 1925 [M1]

Everything that Bajram Bey Curri told me about Ahmet Zog turned out to be true. After Essad Pasha Toptani's assassination in Paris in 1920, Ahmet Zog seized power in Albania under the pretension of following his politics. Ahmet was from an impoverished Bey's family, and had no clan behind him. The others who had one were a nuisance to him. His government tried to get rid of all politically powerful people. Ahmet's regime dissolved Essad Pasha's Party and started to arrest its members.

In 1924, due to an uprising, Ahmet had to escape to Yugoslavia. In 1925, with the help of King Alexander I of Yugoslavia, he returned to Albania. Bajram Bey Curri was killed that year. Because of the help, Ahmet returned the St. Naum Monastery (near Ohrid) to King Alexander I. The Kryeziu family also helped Ahmet Zog to re-enter Albania, as Ceno had married his sister, Nafije Zogu. Despite this, Ceno Bey was assassinated in 1927, likely because he was rumoured to be under the influence of people in Kosovo.

He was serving as Albanian Ambassador to Prague (Czechoslovakia) at the time. On his way to Prague though, he stopped in Dubrovnik, and of course was our guest. He only stayed one day. As if I had a premonition, I told him, "Ceno, why did you consent to leave Albania, your place is in Tiranë". He answered, "Yes, Nush, you are right. I fought to stay, and only agreed to go after they promised me that it would be for a short time". That was the last time we saw him. After Ceno's assassination, the family Kryeziu left Albania and returned to Gjakova, no longer trusting anyone in Ahmet's government.

Ceno Bey Kryeziu, 1925 [M2]

When Ahmet's mother (born Toptani) and sisters passed through Dubrovnik, we often met by chance [Ahmet had by now proclaimed himself King of Albania]. On one such occasion, his mother insisted that we get together as she wanted for her son and I to reconcile our differences. I could not make up my mind regarding the reconciliation, doubting that it would be successful and lasting. It was not so easy for me at the time to move about, having to take care and support nine members of the family: my wife and I, our three daughters and son, my late brother's widow, as well as their son and daughter. I really could not take chances.

Chapter 9: Belgrade

During the world economic crisis of 1929, our business collapsed. There was no more reason for us to stay in Dubrovnik. Palokë came again, and we decided to move to Belgrade. He also came to take Pina and her children back to Albania. Most of the family property in Albania was gone and the rest was diminishing every day. It would be easy to divide in two. Pina refused again, and decided to stay with me and my family. Nine's brother, Lec, wrote to me from Trieste that I should join him there and work for him, thinking Pina would be going back to Albania. But when Pina refused to return, I thanked Lec as we were still a family of nine. Palokë returned to Shkodër and I moved our extended family to Belgrade.

Before I left Dubrovnik, I gave Kolë good references for all the years he had worked for our family, and had been our right hand. With the help of close family friends, I procured for him the job of Dubrovnik representative for the "Boston" shoe factory in Belgrade, where he is now doing very well. That summer, Zina also completed her studies and graduated in the Academy of Commerce. The other children were still in school.

In 1930, after the New Year, I had to go on a business trip for a couple of days. Meanwhile, Zina went to visit a friend of our family, Dr. Maria Vučetić, to see if she could help her find employment. Dr. Vučetić called a banker, Aca Javanović (from Resavac). Quite by chance, this was the bank we had worked with when we had our business partnership in Yugoslavia after World War I. When Aca found out who Zina was, he set her up with employment in an aircraft plant. This plant was actually his enterprise, but went under the name "Rogožarski".

Rogožarski was a carpenter who had worked in Hungary in an aircraft plant. After World War I, he came to Belgrade, as he was Serbian, and suggested to Aca to start a plant in Belgrade. Aca financed it and Rogožarski managed it. Zina started working there in January 1930. In 1934, Aca bought out Rogožarski and converted the business into a share-holding partnership.

I remember it as if it was yesterday, I had just come back from a trip and found quite a rebellion at home. Zina had started to work, against the desires of Nine and Pina. They greeted me with, "It is a shame and a disgrace for a daughter of Shkreli's to work for a living". Even Nine's father, Baba Gasper, had written a harsh letter that Zina's decision to work was a disgrace for the family. Thank God the other children did not pay any attention to this. When Zina came home from work in the evening, a long debate took place.

Zina did not consent to leave her job, explaining that she would give the salary she was receiving to the household. This would help as the living was very expensive to support a family of nine to the degree that our social position required. In Albania, most of the property was lost or sold already, but Nine still had some income from it, which she too gave to the household. Gradually, Nine and Pina got used to the idea as they saw that other girls from good families in Belgrade were also working.

I was not feeling well these days, as the consequences of the internment by the Austro-Hungarian army made me unable to do heavy work. Sometimes I was able to write articles. Friends in the government in Belgrade recommended I make a petition to the government with the following argument: as my original war receipts were lost by the ministry, and because my brother and I had suffered and lost most of our property during the war as a consequence of helping the Serbian army, that I should request a pension for myself as well as my brother's widow. I submitted that application, and in 1934, we got these pensions. They gave two thousand dinars a month for me, and the same for Pina. Zina's salary was another three and a half thousand dinars per month, plus we had Nine's income too. The same year, Zela graduated and started to work as well.

We continued our friendship with the Kryeziu family in Belgrade. Gani Bey spent most of his time there. Hasan Bey was in Gjakova and Said Bey continued his studies in Paris. Their mother was a very interesting and kind lady, and often visited in Belgrade. We spent many occasions with her, remembering the past and planning for the future. With all my heart, I wish Gani the best success in his political endeavours. In the summer of 1935, we (Joseph, Gita, Zana and I) spent six weeks in Gjakova as guests of the Kryeziu family. We were warmly welcomed and had a good time I will always remember.

In the autumn of 1936, Zela married Milan Indić, a young, handsome and good man. She was the first of the children to get married, and it was a great joy for me and Nine. We were happy that the family was growing and that a new household had been established. Milan's brother, Miodrag, was a journalist and the owner of the monthly commercial business magazine, Yugoslovenski Kurir. We had a lot of friends and acquaintances in Belgrade, with the consequence that we had to entertain a lot. The authorities considered us as "emmigrants d'honneur" (honorable emigrants).

I did not go back to Albania. From Belgrade, only Nine and Gita went to Shkodër, and Tiranë, to attend the wedding of Cinë, Nine's cousin and son of Shuk Serreqi. My nephew Ndoci graduated from high school and began preparing for university. In the spring of 1938, Zina got engaged to Bruno Prister. Bruno was also a good, young man, loved by all of us. I got two son-in-laws, and was hopeful for a third.

Before Zina's wedding, Pina told us that she was going to live apart from us as her situation now was quite different. She had the pension I procured for her. Lleshi (the nephew of Lekë Mirash Luca) used to reproached his uncle for not having facilitated his life as I had done for Pina and her children. Ndoci decided to go to the University of Bucarest in Romania. Although Pina did not tell me that he had gotten a scholarship from Albania, I found out from the man that procured it. I never mentioned it to Pina, as she'd used her need to support Ndoci from her pension as a reason for leaving us. So, that summer, she got a separate apartment.

In the autumn, Zina and Bruno got married and it was a great joy for the family. Another family was established. Zina continued to work and she told me that, with Bruno's agreement, she was going to continue to contribute her whole salary to my household until Joseph graduated from university. At the end of 1938, the Ministry of Foreign Affairs summoned Pina and told her that she and her daughter Zana should leave Yugoslavia, as her son had gotten the scholarship from Albania. She came immediately to us (me, Nine and Zina), and we decided that she should let the ministry know that Ndoci had gone against her will in getting the scholarship. The next day I went with Pina to the ministry, and after a lot of discussion, they decided to allow Pina and Zana to remain in Yugoslavia. However, since then, all correspondence between Ndoci and Pina was to be channeled through Zina's address. Ndoci has since left Bucarest and gone to Milan to continue his studies towards an engineering degree.

In the spring of 1939, the cartel of cement industries of Yugoslavia, where Bruno was employed, wanted him to live in Paris and be their representative in the International Cement Concern. Those were days of much worry. If Bruno went, he'd have to take Zina with him, and then we'd have to make do without her income. God bless them though, as they decided to stay. Bruno was able to postpone his appointment for the next term, as representatives were reappointed every four years. By that time, Joseph would have graduated and been able to work. I was afraid that maybe I did wrong by Zina and Bruno, but Zina assured me that she prefered to be near us.

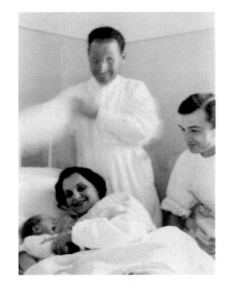

The 19th of April 1939 was a very happy day for all of us, especially Nine and I, as it was the birth of our granddaughter, little Nina [Ninuška / Ninusha / Nineta], Milan and Zela's daughter. I have no words to express the extent of our delight. I wish her all the happiness in the world. God bless her, a very beautiful and cute baby.

Nina & Zela, 1939 [FA]

On the 15th of January 1940, I had a gallstone operation and at 11am, they took me to the operating theatre. It was a day I will always remember. I was very hesitant about this operation as I doubted that I would survive. Thank God, I did. I was not so much afraid for my life, but rather that I felt sorry for the expenses that Zina has had to bear for me in vain. It is still in front of my eyes, the moment when they were transporting me to the operating room. My whole family gathered in front, and it broke my heart as I thought I'd never see them again.

The sanatorium where I was operated on was one of the best in Belgrade. When I woke up after the operation, I could hardly believe that I was still alive. Although I had a private nurse during the night, Gita spent the night after the operation at my bedside. While I was still in the sanatorium, Gita had her appendix removed and she was recovering in the room with me. With my medication, and good care from Nine, I recovered quickly and by summer was quite well again.

Although World War II had started, life was still normal in Yugoslavia. On New Year's Eve 1940, Nine and I went to the Jesuit Church for the Te Deum service to praise God and give thanks for the past year. After church, we went to see our grand-daughter Nina and then went home. I remember this was the first year that I celebrated the Silvester [New Year's Eve] quietly at home. When in Shkodër, we had always celebrated it in a big way. Then in Belgrade, it was usually in the hotels: Excelsior [Mercure] or Srpski Kralj. This year, because of the recent operation, it was best for me to take it easy.

Zina and Bruno invited Gita to go with them to Srpski Kralj, but she declined. Joseph went with his friends from the swimming club, Sever. He was not a member but was on the entertainment committee organizing the party. For the occasion they'd rented space in the Cvijeta Zuzorić Hall in Kalemegdan. Zela and Milan went to celebrate with their friends at Dva Pobratima and Bajlonova Pivara. Gita put Nina to bed.

That night, I could not sleep, thinking of old times and old customs and how much they'd changed since I was born and raised. But, at the same time, I felt peaceful and satisfied in my heart, as we were entering the new year all healthy, safe and sound. Two daughters had married, and there was hope the third would find the man of her choice too. Our son graduated from high school and started his studies in university. Until now he'd not had any bad habits, and had a lot of well brought up friends from good families. I was very satisfied with my two son-in-laws, and immensely happy with out granddaughter, little Nina. She loved me and when she wanted to show me how much, she would stretch her arms very wide.

On the morning of New Year's Day, 1941, Zina came. I told her, "Nine and I are coming in the afternoon to your place". She replied, "No, in the afternoon you are going to rest as I have bought you tickets for the theatre for this evening". God bless them, they wanted to make up for us for having to stay at home on New Year's Eve. Gita was out for the whole day with her friends. Zela and little Nina had lunch with me. Zela came with hands full of presents. In the afternoon, we had a lot of visitors who came to wish us a Happy New Year. After dinner, Joseph left for Kopaonik, a mountain range where the skiing is good, to prepare for the championship that was to take place there soon. At 7:30 in the evening, we went to the theatre at Knežev Spomenik. They were presenting the opera "The Marriage Of Figaro" by Mozart. We had great seats, in the middle of the first row.

Knežev Spomenik Theatre, circa 1940 [PD]

On the 7th of January 1941, I had a restless night and many bad dreams. Early in the morning, incessant ringing of the doorbell woke me up. As the others had not heard it, I went to answer the door. But, before opening the door, I asked who it was. It was Joseph. My heart started to beat rapidly. I knew something bad had happened. When I openned the door, I saw Joseph with two of his friends supporting him. He told me that he had broken his leg.

It was heartbreaking for me to see him in pain. Everybody was instantly awake and helped Joseph to the bed. In the morning, we took him by taxi to the clinic. Thank God he had not broken the bone, only cracked it, but it had to be put in a cast anyway. I let Zina and Bruno know and they came immediately. I did not inform Zela and Milan, as I didn't want to upset them. They were celebrating the Orthodox Christmas (Eastern European Church) with Milan's brother, Miodrag, at their place in Dedinje (in Belgrade). Nine and I wanted to visit with them as well, but Nine stayed with Joseph and I went with Gita.

On the 8th of January 1941, we all (Nine, Pina, Zana, Gita, Zina, Bruno and I) were invited to Zela and Milan's place. Nine didn't want to go and leave him, but Joseph made her. Zela's maid had brought portions of the meal to our house for Joseph and our housemaid. We spent a pleasant evening with little Nina until midnight.

On the 26th of January, we celebrated the anniversary of my operation with a dinner. I invited Zina, Bruno, Zela, Milan, little Nina, Pina, and Zana, and we spent a nice day together. My heart was full of joy to have all my family, that I love so dearly, around me. To think that a year ago, I thought myself a goner. A great satisfaction came over me seeing that not only my wife and children, but also my son-in-laws, were interested in my health. Little Nina constantly sat on my lap. She called me "Baba Nush". When she was with me, she never got cross or cried. She was always happy when I went to see them. When I was leaving, she'd say, "Don't go". It made me very happy that I lived to see at least one grandchild. In the afternoon, my children and son-in-laws decided that all of us should spend the evening at the theatre in Vračar, where the comedy "Kišobranci" [The Umbrella Men] was being shown. We enjoyed the performance very much.

The 19th of March is the name day and birthday of our son, Joseph. We celebrated it with a dinner for the whole family and some friends. We had a great evening, talking and laughing. It was a joy for me to see Joseph at university, being a good student and already a young man. It will be even more joyous when he graduates.

There were rumours that Yugoslavia would also have to enter World War II. Dr. Ciner, our family doctor, advised me to go with my wife to Vnjačka Banja, a well known spa, as it would be good for my health. We did not go right away because we wanted to celebrate Easter with our family. On the 6th of April 1941, the Nazis bombed Belgrade. Damn them. I curse them because they not only ruined my health totally, but destroyed our family unit by scattering us around, not to mention the ruin of the city and other consequences.

When Nazi Germany's army occupied Yugoslavia, they issued a proclamation to all foreigners to return to their countries, or they would be put into prison camps. So Nine, Joseph, Gita, Pina, Zana and I all returned to Shkodër, Albania. Zela, Milan and little Nina remained in Belgrade. Zina and Bruno escaped to Split (a town on the Adriatic coast of Croatia where the cement company Bruno worked for had their head office). Gita found a job in Tiranë. Joseph went to Italy to continue his studies in the University of Milan. So Nine and I remained alone. Poor Nine, alone, and with so much sacrificed because of my illness. Every Saturday, Gita came and stayed until Sunday evening. We loved that. Rosa, granddaughter of my cousin Ndocë and daughter of Ganxhke and Shan Markshteja, was very helpful toward Nine. Nine had always been good to her mother, Ganxhe, and now Rosa was returning the kindness.

Shan Markshteja [M2]

Zina promised to come and see me. As much as I desired it, I was also afraid for her travelling in war time. Thank God we got letters from Joseph, and he wrote that he was well. We also got good news from Zela, Nina and Milan, that they were well. I feel so sorry for my wife, that we are alone. A couple of times, I tried going for a walk, but I was very weak. We still had lots of visitors though.

In November 1942, Zina delighted us with a visit. She stayed for 15 days with us. She never even left the house, so that we could enjoy each other's company as much as possible. The days just flew by. We talked a great deal, but nevertheless, many things remained unsaid. When Gita came, the same was true. We talked until dawn. Zina had to return to Split, so we said our goodbyes. Parting was very sorrowful, with distress caused by the knowledge that this may be the last time we see each other.

[N.B. Although Milan was killed in a car accident in August, Nush was not initially told due to his declining health. During Zina's visit, Nine, fortified by her presence, decided he should be told, but mostly out of fear someone outside the family might express their condolences. Otherwise, she would have preferred to spare him this tragic news.]

I am very sorry for Milan's passing, and worried about Zela and little Nina. I wrote Zela to come as soon as possible so as not to be alone in Belgrade. Every day I am weaker and weaker. I wonder if I would live to see Zela, Nina and Joseph again. Only God knows.

My dear wife Nine, I thank you for all your love you have given to me, for the years you have spent with me in the good and the bad, for all the sacrifices you are making now during my illness. May God in return give you all the best. Gita, Zela, Joseph, Nina, Zina and Bruno, my beloved children, I thank you with all my heart for all the good things you have done for me, for all the love you have given me. Forgive me for not having been able to give you all that I desired. We had so many wonderful plans for your future. God bless you. I bless you and my blessings shall be with you throughout your lives. I entrust the care of your mother to you.

Nush Shkreli-Vata
Shkodër, 1942.

Epilogue 1
By Zina Prister

To our deep sorrow, our father, Nush, passed away on the 15th of December 1942 in Shkodër, Albania. He was surrounded by his wife Nine, his daughter Gita, his son Joseph, and our Kolë [Nikola Paldeda]. His family and friends came to pay their last respects, and he was buried in our family tomb in Shkodër. Thanks to his good intentions, we have, and even more important, his future generations will have, a document of their background and the roots of our family.

In 1939, when father started to write these memoirs, he had just put down the main points of the events as they were taking place. He had intended to elaborate and enrich the details later on. Alas, he passed away at the age of 62, not being able to fulfil this intention. We are immensely thankful for these memoirs, records and roots of the origin of the family, even though it is only the condensed form of the history of the family.

After father's death, Gita took mother [Nine] to live with her in Tiranë (Albania). In August 1942, Zela lost her husband, Milan. This was a very painful loss for her and her daughter Nina, who was only three years old. Gita summoned Zela and Nina to come to Tiranë so as not be alone in Belgrade, which they did in 1943. With the war raging all over Europe, and a disastrous situation on the Balkan Peninsula, partly occupied by Nazi Germany and partly by Fascist Italy, Zela had no choice and made this trip with little Nina. So, in Tiranë, Nine, Nina, Gita and Zela were reunited, and Gita and Zela got jobs.

After the capitulation of Fascist Italy in 1943, Bruno and I joined the Yugoslav National Liberation Army against the Nazis and Fascists. Joseph got involved with the Italian underground and American OSS. In autumn of 1945, we were demobilized. After that, Bruno worked for UNRA [United Nations Relief Agency]. In 1946, Joseph graduated and got his Doctorate Law Diploma.

After the end of World War II, Zela and her daughter managed to leave Albania and returned to Belgrade. Zela found employment there at a bank and held a responsible position. Both countries, Albania and Yugoslavia, were under communist regimes. Bruno and I returned to Zagreb, where he became the commercial manager of the cement factory in Podsused [near Zagreb] until his retirement in 1963. In January 1947, Nine and Gita managed to leave Albania and went to Yugoslavia. Nine went to live in Belgrade with Zela and Nina. Gita went to Zagreb, where Bruno and I were living, and obtained a position as a bank clerk. After Bruno's retirement in 1963, he became a consultant for the Yugoslav Cement Association in Zagreb until his death on the 22nd of September 1987.

There's no need to write about how it was after World War II and how the war devastated Europe, as this is already described in history books. Because of that situation, there was a lot of emigration from Europe to North and South America, Australia and New Zealand. This time not only did the working class emigrate, but also the politicians, intellectuals, specialists, and people with means. All were escaping the ruined and destroyed Europe, communism or other problems.

Gita remained in Zagreb until 1950. Before she left, Nine, Zela and Nina joined us in Zagreb, so all but Joseph were present to say our goodbyes. It was a painful parting, wondering when and if we would see each other again. Gita went to Trieste, then an International Zone. In the spring of 1951, she went from there through Germany to Canada. First she went to Winnipeg, and then after a couple of months, she came to Toronto. Gita was the first in the family to emigrate to Canada. It took great courage and determination to make such a move.

After Gita sent the appropriate papers to Joseph, he was able to emigrate to Toronto, on the 2nd of January 1952. In November 1953, Zela did the same, leaving by way of Germany with her daughter and coming to Toronto as well. Mother [Nine] came to stay with me. In 1955, Joseph married Neda Fisher and on the 7th of September 1956, Zela married again, to Svetislav Teodosijevich. After a few temporary jobs, Zela obtained a permanent position at the Bank Of Montreal where she stayed until retirement.

In 1963, mother [Nine] also emigrated to Canada, and stayed with Zela and her husband, and sometimes with Joseph and his family. Joseph officially changed his name from Shkreli to Skelly. On the 20th of June 1964, Nina married John Richard Emery. They had two sons: James and Rob [Robert]. Mother [Nine] died on the 23rd of May 1974, and was buried in the York Cemetary in North York.

After Bruno's death, I was invited to join the family in Canada. Zela arranged the papers for me and so in 1988, I also emigrated to Toronto. As of the 11th of September 1992, I became a Canadian Citizen.

Zina Prister
born Shkreli-Vata
Toronto, 1994.

Epilogue 2
By Rob Emery

Since the Memoirs were translated, Joseph passed away on the 20th of February 2004. Zina passed away on the 12th of February 2007. My grandmother, Zela, passed away on the 24th of April in 2011. Gita passed away on the 25th of October 2012. My grandfather, Svetislav, passed away on the 14th of September in 2014. My father, John, passed away on the 7th of May 2016.

Rob Emery
Toronto, 2021.

Zela, Rob & Nine [FA]

Appendix: Family Trees

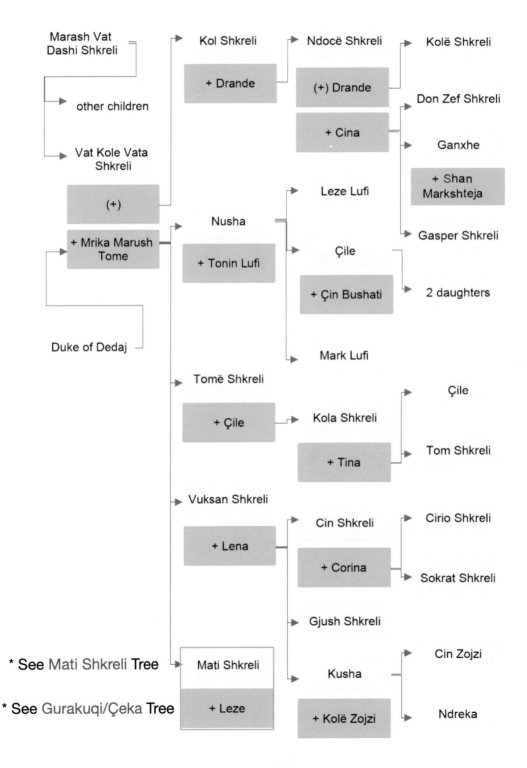

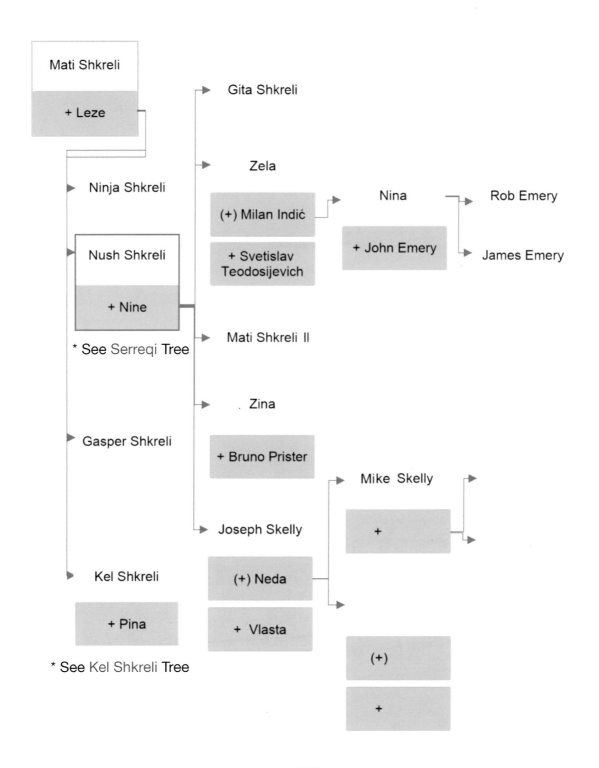

Mati Shkreli

+ Leze

Gita Shkreli

Zela

(+) Milan Indić

Nina

Rob Emery

+ John Emery

James Emery

+ Svetislav
Teodosijevich

Ninja Shkreli

Nush Shkreli

+ Nine

* See Serreqi Tree

Mati Shkreli II

Zina

Gasper Shkreli

+ Bruno Prister

Mike Skelly

+

Joseph Skelly

(+) Neda

Kel Shkreli

+ Pina

+ Vlasta

(+)

+

* See Kel Shkreli Tree

109

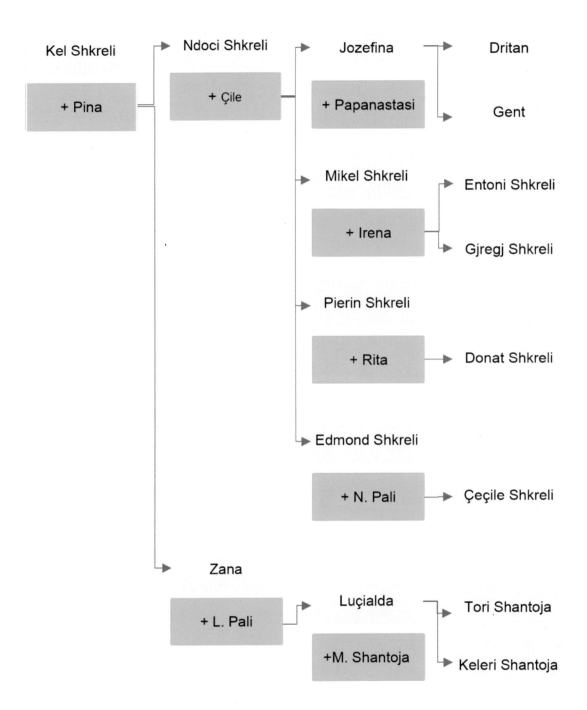

Kel Shkreli

+ Pina

Ndoci Shkreli

+ Çile

Jozefina

+ Papanastasi

Dritan

Gent

Mikel Shkreli

+ Irena

Entoni Shkreli

Gjregj Shkreli

Pierin Shkreli

+ Rita

Donat Shkreli

Edmond Shkreli

+ N. Pali

Çeçile Shkreli

Zana

+ L. Pali

Luçialda

+M. Shantoja

Tori Shantoja

Keleri Shantoja

110

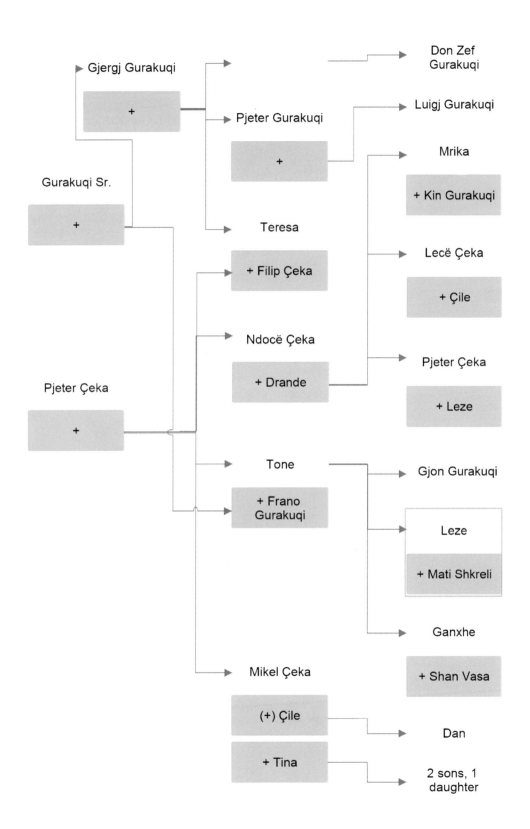

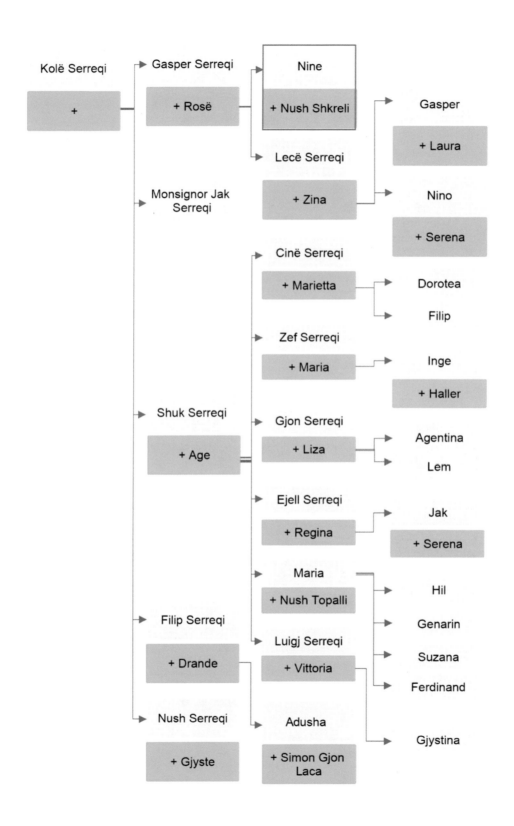

Kolë Serreqi

\+

Gasper Serreqi

\+ Rosë

Nine

\+ Nush Shkreli

Lecë Serreqi

\+ Zina

Gasper

\+ Laura

Nino

\+ Serena

Monsignor Jak
Serreqi

Cinë Serreqi

\+ Marietta

Dorotea

Filip

Zef Serreqi

\+ Maria

Inge

\+ Haller

Shuk Serreqi

\+ Age

Gjon Serreqi

\+ Liza

Agentina

Lem

Ejell Serreqi

\+ Regina

Jak

\+ Serena

Maria

\+ Nush Topalli

Hil

Genarin

Suzana

Ferdinand

Filip Serreqi

\+ Drande

Luigj Serreqi

\+ Vittoria

Nush Serreqi

\+ Gjyste

Adusha

\+ Simon Gjon
Laca

Gjystina

About The Author & Contributors

Although the youngest of the children, Nush Mati Shkreli-Vata was interested in listening to the grownups when they talked, especially about stories of the origin and descendants of the family and their way of living. Because of this, the family gave him the duty and responsibility to collect documents, records and information about the family, both written and through word of mouth. To his regret, when the Austro-Hungarian army occupied the family's hometown of Shkodër (Albania) during World War I, they took possession of his house, and burned many of these documents.

His sister (Ninja) was also interested in Albanian history and customs. She collected whatever she could of country songs, jokes, stories and customs of Malcija and of Geg [Gegnia / Gegëria - Northern Albania, where people speak the Gheg dialect]. Sadly, these were among things lost during the Balkan War of 1913 when a bomb hit part of the house. Nush felt he couldn't make a complete book of the family and its origin without the documents lost during the Balkan War and WWI, but wanted to leave to his children, and the children of his brother (Kel), these memoirs and records so that they could at least have a view of the origin of the family.

This book was originally written by Nush in 1938 - 1942, and later translated ad litteram from Albanian to English in 1992-1994 by his daughter, Zina Prister (born Shkreli-Vata). It was edited for clarity in 2020-2021 by his great-grandson, Rob Emery. Rob also added maps and photos from family albums and online sources. One large source was the Marubi Museum, containing the photography of Pietro & Kel Marubi, among others. All the black and white photos in these memoirs were restored and colourized by Rob.

The Marubi photographers [M1]: Pietro (left - original, right - restored & colourized).

The Marubi photographers [M1]: Kel (left - original, right - colourized).

Nush was born in 1880 and died in 1942, in Shkodër, Albania. Zina was born in 1909 in Shkodër, and died in 2007 in Toronto, Canada. Rob was born in 1970 in Toronto and is hopefully still alive.

Rob Emery [FA]

CPSIA information can be obtained
at www.ICGtesting.com
Printed in the USA
LVRC080035281021
701772LV00005B/38